OFFICERS & SOLDIERS of the

ARTILLERY
1786-1815
THE GRIBEAUVAL SYSTEM

Volume II.
The Horse Artillery and the Artillery Train

Ludovic LETRUN
and Jean-Marie MONGIN

Translated from the French by Alan McKAY

Histoire & Collections

FROM MOBILE ARTILLERY TO HORSE ARTILLERY

1792 – the Birth of the Mobile Artillery

A decree issued on 29 April 1792 created nine horse artillery companies, two of which were attached to the first two regiments; the remaining five were attached to each of the following regiments. These companies were only mounted in times of war.

The rules for the uniform that the artillerymen designated to join these nine companies wore were drawn up in June of the same year. They had a similar coat to that of the gunners in the foot regiments to which the companies were attached. Besides the coat button bore their regimental number.

The epaulets had scarlet wool fringes. The waistcoat was made of blue cloth lined with white caddis and had two rows of little buttons. A greatcoat, also made of blue cloth, together with leather gloves was issued to the soldiers.

The Hungarian-style breeches were also made of blue cloth, its braid and cords were made of red wool. A stable waistcoat and overbreeches made of woven blue cloth were also supplied.

Headgear consisted of the varnished felt helmet, the same model as supplied to the infantry; a plume and a scarlet wool tuft completed the uniform. A foot artillery model forage cap was also supplied.

THE HORSE ARTILLERY COMPANY IN 1792

1 captain commanding	30 first-gunners
1 second captain,	30 second- gunners
1 first lieutenant,	among which:
1 second lieutenant	1 blacksmith
1 sergeant-major	1 saddler
3 sergeants	1 boot-maker
1 corporal-fourrier,	2 woodworkers
3 corporals	2 ironworkers
3 appointees,	(6 served on foot)
3 artificers	
3 mounted trumpeters	81 men in all of whom
21 men were mounted	75 were mounted

The trumpeter's coat was the same as the drummers' in the foot artillery, ornamented with specific Horse Artillery items.

A special short sabre was issued but the Hussar's sabre was also to be found. The Light Cavalry type belt made of whitened leather, and the Hungarian-style boots completed the Horse Artilleryman's gear.

The saddle was French, covered with a sheepskin schabrack festooned with scarlet; the portmanteau was made of blue cloth with scarlet braid. The officers had a blue schabrack festooned with scarlet and decorated with a gold stripe.

When the Horse Artillery was created, this modified the arm's role on the battlefield. It became autonomous and no longer depended on the infantry when serving. In February 1793, the number of horse artillery companies was increased to twenty.

1794 – an undeniable success

The trend for horse artillery resulted in the nine companies being quickly changed into just as many regiments on 7 February 1794. The uniform was also substantially modified, changing these artillerymen into dashing hussars. The blue cloth dolman in theory had three rows of 15 buttons, but could also have five like that of the hussars; the collar was blue, the facings and the tresses were scarlet; the sash was blue with scarlet knots.

The shako was also the one used by the hussars of the period. Without a visor and slightly conical, it was made of black felt, covered with a scarlet flame. The cord and the plume were the same colour.

The *sabretache* covered with blue cloth was also edged with leather and with a wide scarlet stripe, lined on the inside with scarlet cord. The decoration was made of copper and represented two crossed cannon with the regimental number above and a grenade under them.

The armament and the equipment were those issued to the *"Chasseurs à Cheval"*. The trumpeters had their own uniform with the colours reversed, as was the custom in the cavalry.

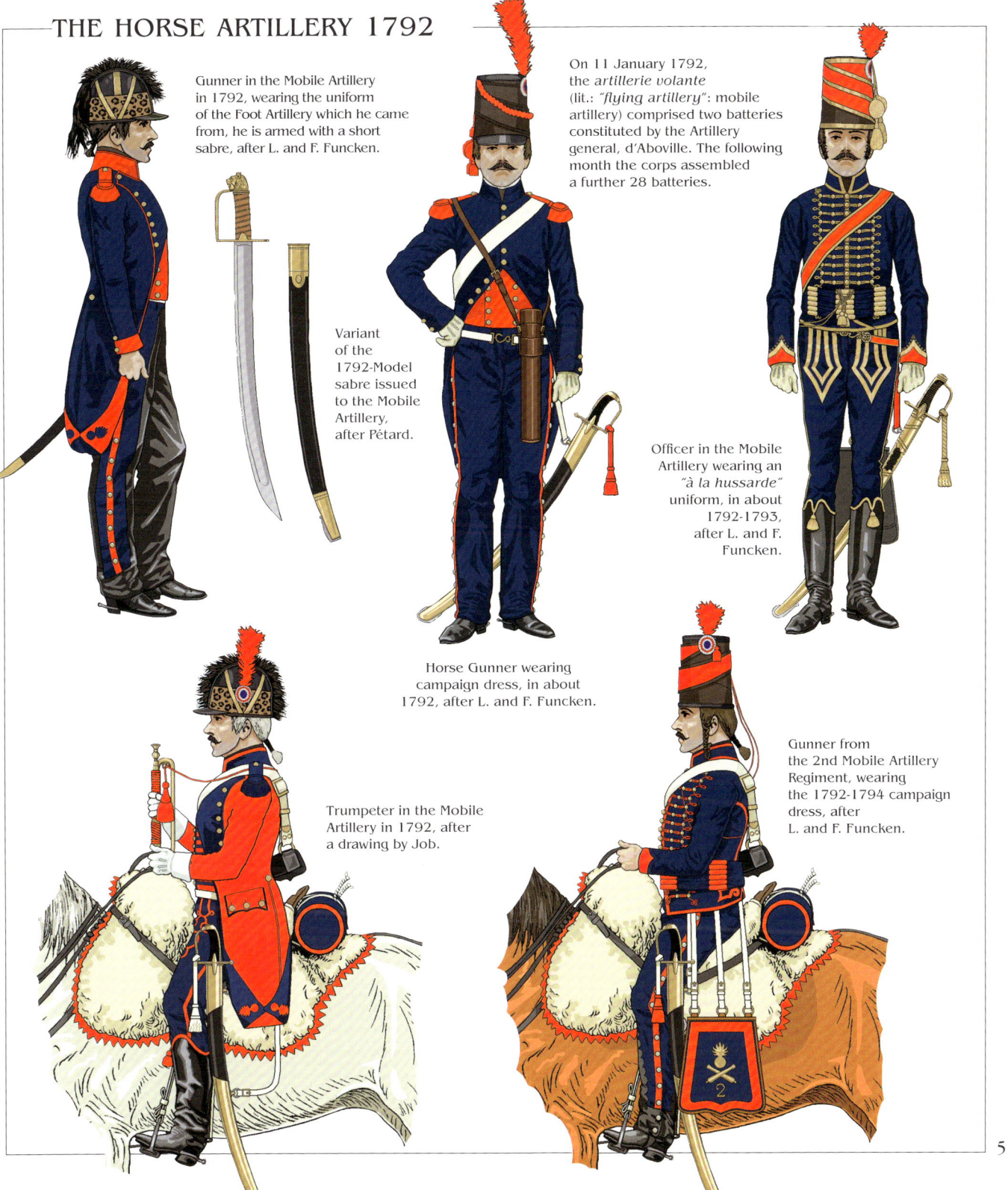

THE HORSE ARTILLERY 1792

Gunner in the Mobile Artillery in 1792, wearing the uniform of the Foot Artillery which he came from, he is armed with a short sabre, after L. and F. Funcken.

Variant of the 1792-Model sabre issued to the Mobile Artillery, after Pétard.

On 11 January 1792, the *artillerie volante* (lit.: "flying artillery": mobile artillery) comprised two batteries constituted by the Artillery general, d'Aboville. The following month the corps assembled a further 28 batteries.

Officer in the Mobile Artillery wearing an "à la hussarde" uniform, in about 1792-1793, after L. and F. Funcken.

Horse Gunner wearing campaign dress, in about 1792, after L. and F. Funcken.

Trumpeter in the Mobile Artillery in 1792, after a drawing by Job.

Gunner from the 2nd Mobile Artillery Regiment, wearing the 1792-1794 campaign dress, after L. and F. Funcken.

> ### THE HORSE ARTILLERY REGIMENT
>
> In 1794, the Horse Artillery Regiment consisted of a headquarters and six companies.
>
> **THE HEADQUARTERS**
> 1 brigade commander
> 1 squadron commander
> 1 quarter-master
> 1 adjutant officer
> 1 adjutant NCO
> 1 brigadier trumpeter
> 1 vet
> 1 master worker saddler
> 1 master worker tailor
> 1 master worker boot maker
>
> **THE HORSE ARTILLERY COMPANY**
> 1 captain
> 1 first lieutenant
> 2 sous-lieutenants
> 1 *maréchal des logis chef*
> 4 *maréchaux-des-logis*
> 1 brigadier *fourrier*
> 2 trumpeters
> 30 first gunners
> 36 second gunners
> 4 woodworkers
> 4 ironworkers
>
> *The latter were not mounted*

In May 1795, the horse artillery comprised eight regiments. The make up of each regiment did not change except for the sous-lieutenants who were replaced by second-lieutenants.

At the end of 1799, the artillery corps comprised a headquarters (226 officers) of eight foot regiments (each with twenty companies), eight horse regiments (each with six companies), twelve companies of workers, 32 brigades of craftsmen (60 men) and two battalions of pontoneers.

In 1801 the number of horse regiments was increased to six.

1801-1810 – a deliberate development

The First Consul decided to replace the mirliton shako by a more modern shako with a crown and a hatband. At first issued to the hussars this cap had a visor ringed with copper and scaled copper chinstraps. The cockade was held up in place by a little braid. Saltire hooks on the sides of the shako held the braided cordons with scarlet tassel and flounders. A scarlet plume completed the ensemble. The cartridge case with a flap was decorated with two crossed cannon made of brass. The cartridge case belt was that of the hussars but was also the one worn by the infantry.

In 1804, the horse artillery had six regiments, organised into six companies. A seventh depot company was added in 1809. The companies from the same regiment were spread out as a general rule among the divisions and the army corps, in three 10-gun divisions for the three infantry divisions and one six-gun division for the cavalry. The corps thus shared out five foot artillery companies and one horse Artillery Company among its infantry, pool and cavalry units.

From 1804 to 1812, the full dress clothing article was the dolman but the long coat from the second uniform, which was common to all the cavalry corps wearing the dolman, was often worn for campaign dress and gradually replaced the hussar-style dolman. It was only in 1811 that the regulations stipulated that it was to replace the dolman before it was itself replaced by the habit-veste in 1812.

On 25 April 1806, the gunners received an An-XI model sabre, like the hussars at the same period. In 1810, the Horse Artillery shako which dated back to the beginning of the period was replaced by the hussars' shako.

By decree dated 18 August 1810 and for several months, both companies of Horse Artillery in the Dutch army were attached to the French army and formed the backbone of the 7th Horse Artillery Regiment. As it was impossible to get the regiment up to strength, it was disbanded and the two companies were sent to the 1st and 4th Regiments.

From Bardin's Regulation to the *Fleur de Lys*

In the 1812 Regulations, the "Light Artillery" uniform was the one prescribed for the *"Chasseurs à Cheval"*, but made from dark blue cloth with scarlet distinctives. The habit-veste facings were pointed with scarlet, and open underneath. The turnbacks were scarlet and had blue grenades. The pockets were situated inside the folds and had *"à la Soubise"* flaps. The collar was blue without piping. The lapels were blue with scarlet piping.

The trumpeters underwent the same uniform change and kept the contrary colours. There was a grenade on the turnback.

In 1813, the 1st, 2nd and 3rd Regiments received a seventh company, thus bringing the number of companies to eight, counting the depot company. The Horse Artillery had a blue habit-veste (eight big buttons, 22 medium ones, 3 hooks on the collar, 13 hooks on the

(continued on page 20)

THE HORSE ARTILLERY 1792-1796

When the first Mobile Artillery batteries were created, the Gunners, who were transported on the new Wurst ammunition caissons, kept some of the uniform items belonging to their comrades on foot, but used the breeches and boots of the Light Cavalry.

Horse Gunner, in about 1792, after Rousselot.

Mounted Gunner in 1792, after Pétard.

Maréchal-des-logis in the Mobile Artillery wearing full dress, in about 1792-1794. He is carrying the *chasseurs à cheval* sabre, far more suitable than the short sabre (reconstitution).

Trumpeter in the Mobile Artillery, in about 1792-1796, after L. and F. Funcken.

Mounted Gunner in marching dress, in about 1792-1796 (reconstitution).

1793-1796

Gunner in the Light Artillery, in about 1793-1794, after an engraving by Seele. The coat is fastened with brass buttons and the overbreeches are edged with two scarlet stripes.

Horse Gunner, in about 1793-1794, wearing a Dragoon's helmet, after Seele.

Horse Gunner, in about 1793-1794, after an engraving by Seele. He is still wearing the Foot Artillery uniform with Cavalry of the Line boots.

On 7 March 1795, the Light Artillery was regrouped into 8 six-company regiments.

Officer from the Light Artillery wearing full dress, in about 1796, after old engravings.

Barrel scarf worn with the "à la hussarde" uniform, with skeins of blue cord and scarlet double loops.

Gunner from the 1st Light Artillery Regiment wearing full dress in 1794 after L. and F. Funcken.

1795-1800

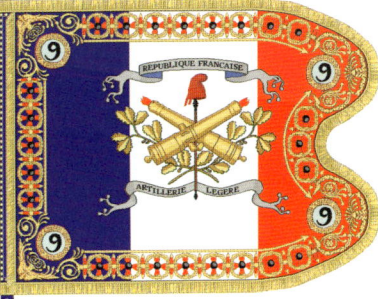

In the centre, oak leaves surround two cannon embroidered in gold over a pike on top of which was a red Phrygian cap.

The regimental number is reproduced in the corners in black on a silver background. Silver stripes bear black captions with REPUBLIQUE FRANCAISE at the top and ARTILLERIE LEGERE at the bottom. The cloth, measuring 29.13 by 39.37 inches, was nailed to the 86.61 in blue tourneying lance. The 40.94 inch tricolour sash was knotted round the bronze pike with the 21.65 in cord made of silver thread and blue and scarlet silk thread.
(Musée de l'Armée)

1795-model Pennant, attributed to the 9th Horse Artillery Regiment, which remained unused. The cloth was made of tricolour double damask, with an acanthus edge and a gold thread fringe.

Brigadier wearing a red waistcoat, in about 1798, after Rigo.

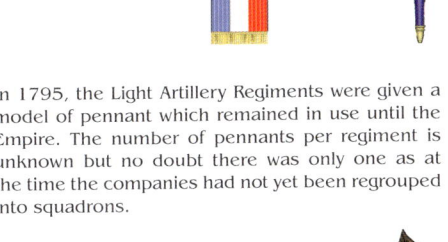

In 1795, the Light Artillery Regiments were given a model of pennant which remained in use until the Empire. The number of pennants per regiment is unknown but no doubt there was only one as at the time the companies had not yet been regrouped into squadrons.

Colonel Sorbier, commanding the 3rd Light Artillery Regiment, in about 1795-1800, after a period engraving, coloured by Job.

Brigadier Pennant-Bearer, from the 1st Company of the Fifth Regiment, in about 1798-1799, after Rigo. On this pennant, the Phrygian cap is tricolour and the oak leaves plain (Charrié).

1795-1800

Horse Gunner, in about 1798-1800, wearing a coat with two shoulder flaps, after a Plate by Knötel.

Horse Gunner during the Italian campaign, after Lejeune.

Horse Gunner in 1799, according to Knötel. The coat worn is still that of the Foot Artillery, with cuff flaps and big pockets ornamented with four buttons.

Gunner in the 1st Light Artillery Regiment in 1795 after Philippoteaux.

Officer in the 1st Artillery Regiment wearing a superb Hussar's uniform, in about 1798-1799, after a contemporary drawing.

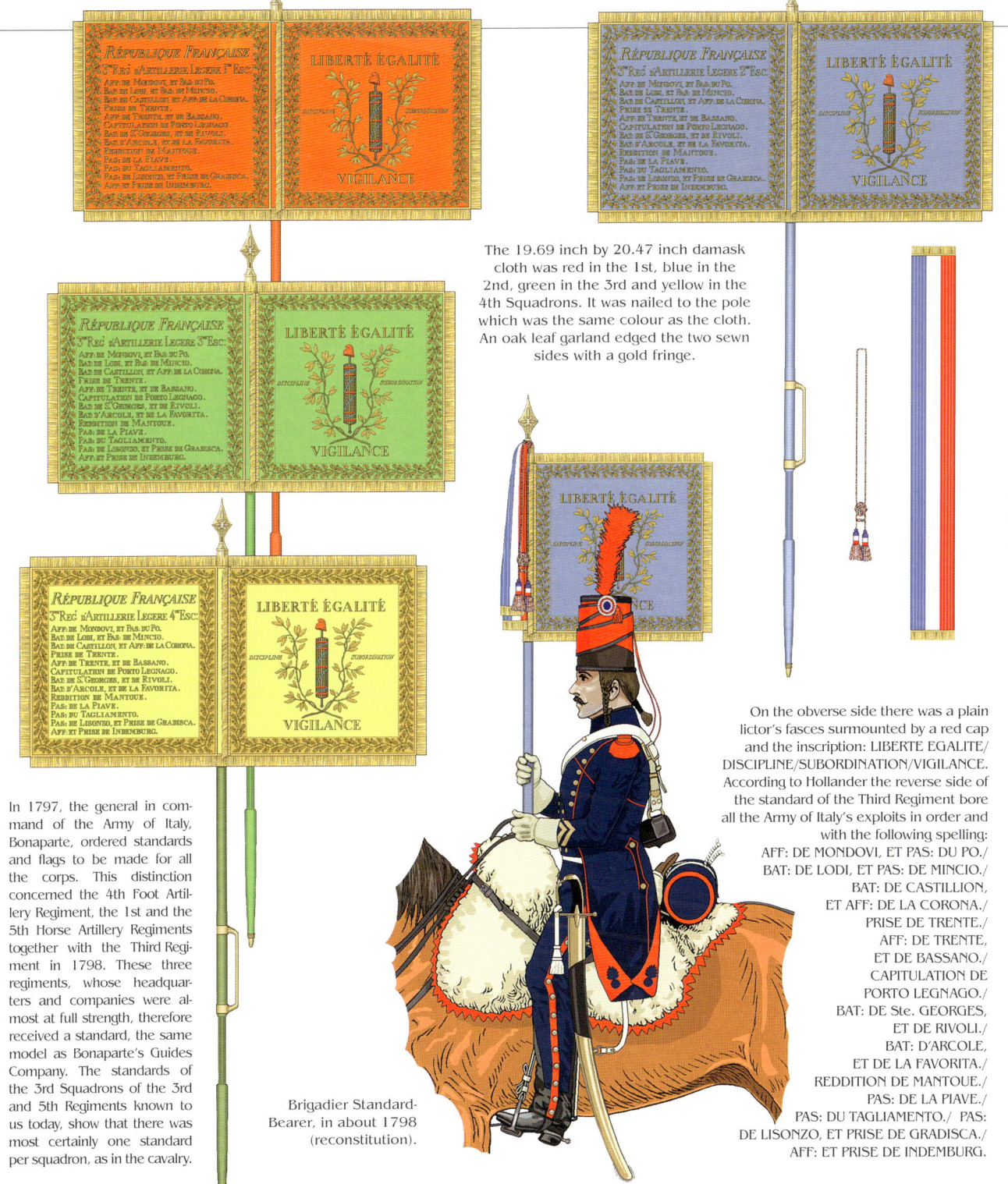

The 19.69 inch by 20.47 inch damask cloth was red in the 1st, blue in the 2nd, green in the 3rd and yellow in the 4th Squadrons. It was nailed to the pole which was the same colour as the cloth. An oak leaf garland edged the two sewn sides with a gold fringe.

In 1797, the general in command of the Army of Italy, Bonaparte, ordered standards and flags to be made for all the corps. This distinction concerned the 4th Foot Artillery Regiment, the 1st and the 5th Horse Artillery Regiments together with the Third Regiment in 1798. These three regiments, whose headquarters and companies were almost at full strength, therefore received a standard, the same model as Bonaparte's Guides Company. The standards of the 3rd Squadrons of the 3rd and 5th Regiments known to us today, show that there was most certainly one standard per squadron, as in the cavalry.

Brigadier Standard-Bearer, in about 1798 (reconstitution).

On the obverse side there was a plain lictor's fasces surmounted by a red cap and the inscription: LIBERTE EGALITE/DISCIPLINE/SUBORDINATION/VIGILANCE. According to Hollander the reverse side of the standard of the Third Regiment bore all the Army of Italy's exploits in order and with the following spelling:
AFF: DE MONDOVI, ET PAS: DU PO./
BAT: DE LODI, ET PAS: DE MINCIO./
BAT: DE CASTILLION,
ET AFF: DE LA CORONA./
PRISE DE TRENTE./
AFF: DE TRENTE,
ET DE BASSANO./
CAPITULATION DE
PORTO LEGNAGO./
BAT: DE Ste. GEORGES,
ET DE RIVOLI./
BAT: D'ARCOLE,
ET DE LA FAVORITA./
REDDITION DE MANTOUE./
PAS: DE LA PIAVE./
PAS: DU TAGLIAMENTO./ PAS:
DE LISONZO, ET PRISE DE GRADISCA./
AFF: ET PRISE DE INDEMBURG.

1798-1800

The Light Artillery which embarked for the Egyptian Expedition brought together several companies from the 3rd, 4th, 5th and 8th Regiments, a total of 485 men. The Gunners disembarked without their mounts except for a few draught horses, which were not to be found in Egypt.

Maréchal-des-logis from the Light Artillery, in about 1798-1799, in the uniform they wore to embark for Egypt, after Boisselier.

Light Gunner in Egypt in 1799, according to *Ordonnateur* Daure's correspondence.

Light Gunner in Egypt, in about 1799-1800, riding a horse requisitioned locally.

Gunner, First Class in the 5th Light Artillery Regiment wearing campaign dress in 1799, after Rigo. He is wearing the new shako designed at Boulaq with a clasped peak. He is armed with a blunderbuss taken off the body of a Mameluke.

Light Gunner at the Battle of the Pyramids, after Lejeune.

1801-1806

Trumpeter in a Horse Artillery Regiment, in about 1804-1805, after Seele.

Trumpeter in a Horse Artillery Regiment in 1805, after Wolz.

Maréchal-des-logis in the Horse Artillery in 1805, after Wolz.

Gunner, First Class wearing campaign dress, in about 1804-1806 (reconstitution).

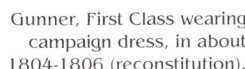

Barrel-sash worn during the Consulate and the Empire, with scarlet cords and blue loops.

Dolman seen from behind, made of dark blue cloth lined with natural-coloured canvas, with a flat cord and scarlet braid. The front was decorated with 18 rows of three brass buttons. Normally there was only one shoulder flap in the shape of a trefoil, on the left.

Gunner wearing stable dress or fatigues from 1801 to 1812 (reconstitution).

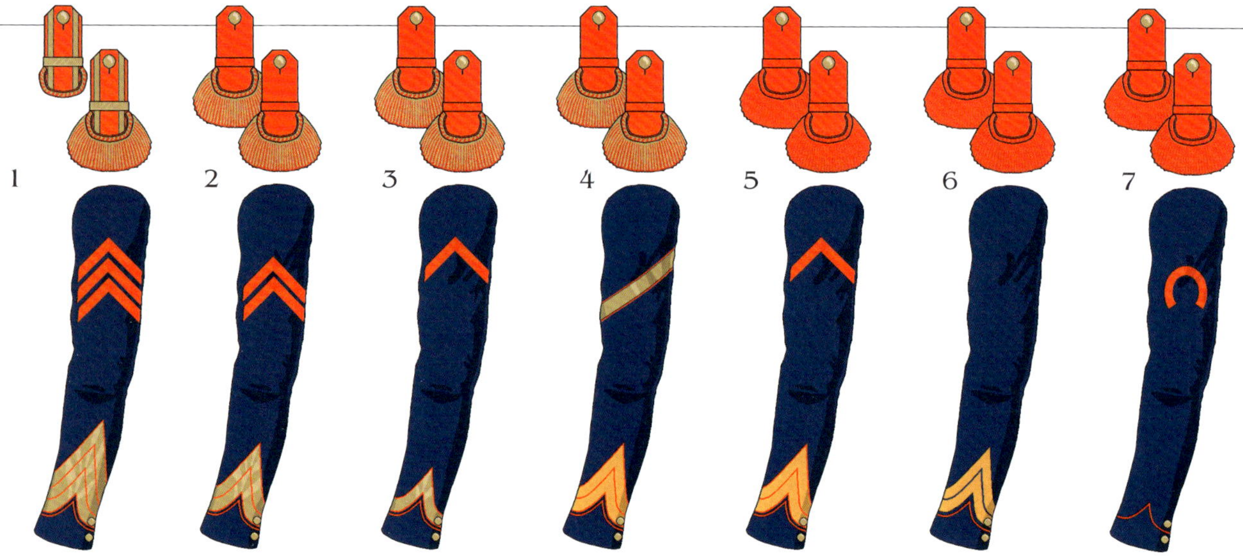

Top, from left to right.
Rank markings on the dolmans, jackets and coats belonging to the ordinary soldiers and NCOs with seniority chevrons made of scarlet braid
(3 chevrons: 20 years', 2 chevrons: 15 years', 1 chevron: 10 years' service).

1. *Adjudant sous-officer*: 3 gold stripes edged with red over the facings, 1 scarlet epaulette and 1 scarlet contra-epaulette with two gold lines with gold and red fringes.
2. *Maréchal-des-logis chef*: 2 gold stripes edged with red over the facings and 2 scarlet epaulettes with scarlet and gold fringes.
3. *Maréchal-des-logis*: 1 gold stripe edged with gold above the facings and two scarlet epaulettes with scarlet and gold fringes.
4. *Brigadier-Fourrier*: 2 aurora stripes edged with red above the facings, 1 gold stripe edged with red on each arm and two scarlet and gold fringes.
5. *Brigadier*: 2 aurora stripes edged with red above the facings and two scarlet epaulettes.
6. *Gunner, First Class*: 2 aurora stripes above the left facing and two scarlet epaulettes.
7. *Maréchal-Ferrant* (blacksmith): 1 scarlet stripe shaped like a horseshoe on each sleeve and 2 scarlet epaulettes.

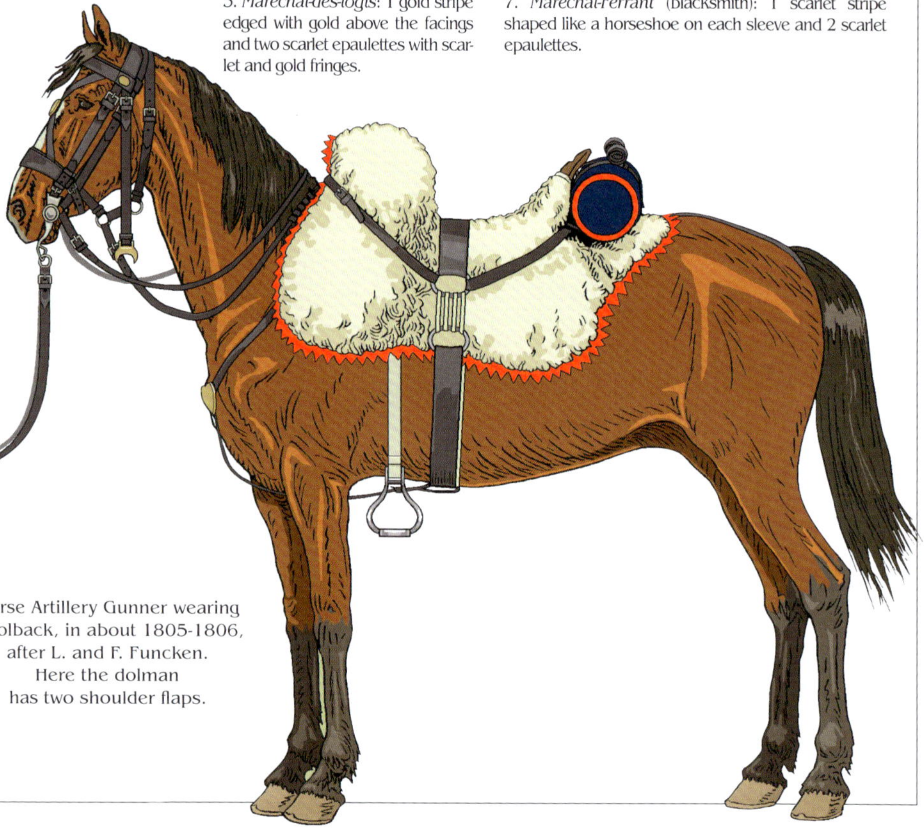

Horse Artillery Gunner wearing a colback, in about 1805-1806, after L. and F. Funcken. Here the dolman has two shoulder flaps.

1805-1815

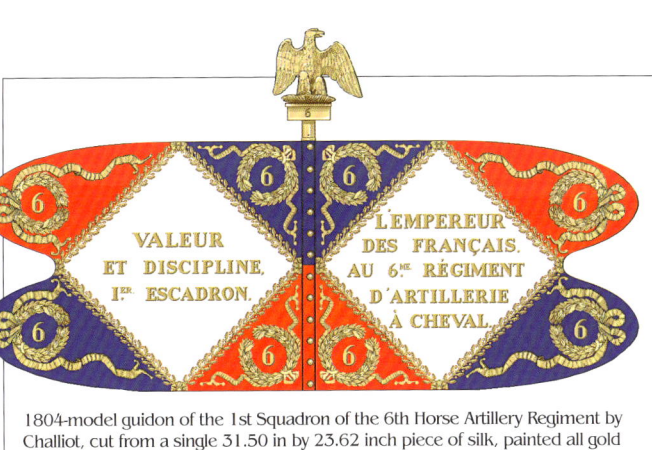

1804-model guidon of the 1st Squadron of the 6th Horse Artillery Regiment by Challiot, cut from a single 31.50 in by 23.62 inch piece of silk, painted all gold with brown shading. The reverse side bears the inscription: L'EMPEREUR/DES FRANCAIS./ AU 6.ME REGIMENT/D'ARTILLERIE/A CHEVAL and on the obverse side VALEUR/ET DISCIPLINE,/ 1.ER ESCADRON. *(Musée de l'Armée Paris)*

First model of bronze eagle with the regimental number on the base. Each regiment received three eagles in 1804.

1812-model tricolour standard of the 4th Horse Artillery Regiment made of a double silk 21.65 inch square with gold embroidery and fringes. After 1811, all the Regiments only had a single eagle, handed out progressively and entrusted to a lieutenant or sous-lieutenant standard-bearer.

The obverse bore the inscription L'EMPEREUR/NAPOLEON/AU 4ME REGIMENT/D'ARTILLERIE/A CHEVAL (the Emperor Napoleon to the 4th Artillery Regiment), and the reverse bore the names of the battles where the regiments had distinguished themselves, for the 1st with WAGRAM, the 2nd with ULM/AUSTERLITZ/IENA/FRIEDLAND/ESSLING/WAGRAM, the 3rd with ULM/AUSTERLITZ/IENA/EYLAU/FRIEDLAND/ESSLING/WAGRAM, the 4th with ESSLING/WAGRAM, the 5th with ULM/AUSTERLITZ/IENA/EYLAU/FRIEDLAND/ESSLING/WAGRAM. The other regiments, no doubt, never received this model of standard.

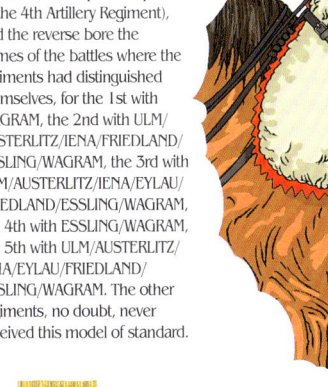

Maréchal-des-logis chef pennant-bearer in the 5th Horse Artillery Regiment, in about 1804-1806 (reconstitution).

1815-model standard of the 4th Horse Artillery Regiment. When the Emperor distributed the eagles on the Champ de Mars on 1 June 1815, only 4 Horse Artillery Regiments received the emblem. The standard was a double silk 21.65 by 21.65 inch square with gold embroidery and fringes. The obverse side and the reverse side both bore the same inscriptions as in 1812. A sash was knotted with a gold cord to the blue pole under the second model of eagle.

During the First Restoration a new white standard bearing the King's Arms was made for four Horse Artillery Regiments. (Reconstitution after Hollander).

It was to have been the Cavalry model, with LE ROI/AU 1ER REGt/D'ARTILLERIE/A CHEVAL (the King to the 1st Horse Artillery Regiment) inscribed on the obverse side.

1804-1808

Horse Artillery Officer wearing campaign dress and a frock coat with a rotunda cape with gold stripes, in about 1804-1808, after Rousselot.

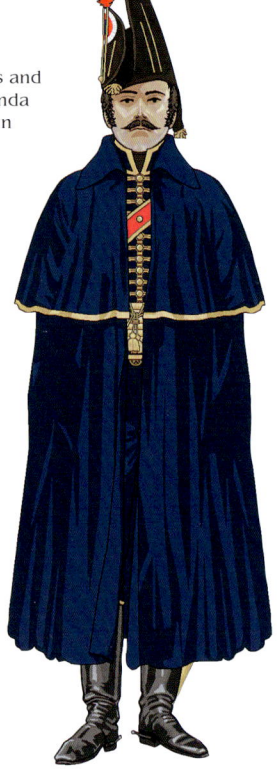

Horse Artillery Officer wearing an overcoat with a turned-down collar and a gold-striped rotunda cape over his full dress, in about 1804-1808 after Rousselot.

The blue overcoat was used by ordinary soldiers from the beginning of the Empire, as confirmed by certain clothing lists.

Captain Noël, in the 1st Horse Artillery Regiment, wearing rather fanciful social dress in Naples, in 1807.

He is wearing nankeen breeches, red morocco boots and Polish headdress, after a period document.

Horse Artillery Officer wearing social dress, in about 1804-1811, after Rousselot. The breeches and the stockings could be either black or white depending on the season. The uniform comprised an overcoat decorated with epaulettes, and nankeen breeches without embroidery.

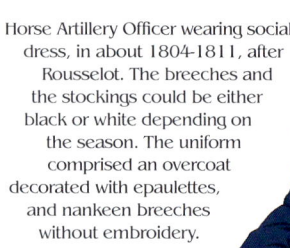

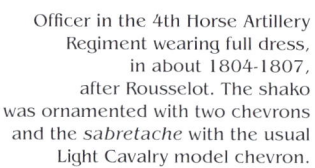

Officer in the 4th Horse Artillery Regiment wearing full dress, in about 1804-1807, after Rousselot. The shako was ornamented with two chevrons and the *sabretache* with the usual Light Cavalry model chevron.

(continued from page 6)
lapels); the blue collar and the lapels had scarlet piping; the scarlet facings were pointed with blue piping. The red epaulets had fringes. The lengthwise pockets with three points and three large buttons were simulated by scarlet piping.

The turnbacks and the epaulet bands were scarlet with blue piping. The turnback ornaments comprised a *"fleur de lys"* and a scarlet grenade.

The buttons were yellow and similar to those in the Foot Artillery. The sleeveless waistcoat was made of blue cloth, fastened with 10 medium-sized buttons. The stable jacket was made of blue cloth, with a blue collar, facings and epaulets with 15 medium-sized buttons.

The trousers were made of serge with a flat scarlet tress. The riding breeches were made of blue cloth and edged with red and had calfskin like the cavalry. They were fastened by 18 bone buttons.

The greatcoat with sleeves and a rotunda cape was blue; it had a standing collar and was fastened with two flaps.

The portmanteau was round, made of blue cloth with a scarlet grenade surrounded by a stripe of the same colour at each end.

THE HORSE ARTILLERY REGIMENT

The Horse Artillery Regiment at the height of the Empire was made up of a headquarters and seven companies, eight after 1813.

THE HEADQUARTERS
1 colonel
1 major
2 squadron commanders
1 quarter-master
1 adjutant major
1 surgeon major
2 adjutant NCOs
1 brigadier trumpeter
1 vet
4 masterworkers

THE HORSE ARTILLERY COMPANY
1 first captain en premier
1 second captain
1 first lieutenant
1 second lieutenant
1 *maréchal-des-logis chef*
4 *maréchaux-des-logis*
1 *fourrier*
4 brigadiers
4 artificers
2 trumpeters
12 *(about)* first class gunners
36 *(about)* second-class gunners

A Horse Artillery company consisted of six guns (of which four were 8-pounders and two six-inch howitzers), two spare gun carriages (one for the cannon and one for the howitzer), fourteen caissons (eight for the cannon, six for the howitzers), three carts, and two forges. This made a total of twenty-seven carriages drawn by more than 220 horses. Eighty men looked after the train and about 120 served the guns.

THE ARTILLERY TRAIN

Transporting the artillery pieces, the caissons and the equipment was carried out by "civil companies" for far too long. The motivation and the courage of the wagoners in the face of the enemy were often more than shaky.

On 3 January 1800, without renouncing his Egyptian ideas, the First Consul decided to create a military artillery train. The corps was made up of five-company battalions.

The elite company was traditionally attached to the Horse Artillery; the four ordinary companies were attached to the Foot Artillery (the first three) and to the depot.

The 4 August 1801 Decree organised this new part of the French army once and for all. The Artillery Train was made up of eight battalions with six 76-man companies. The elite company disappeared.

The strength of the company rose progressively to an average of 100 drivers (generally between 95 and 120), commanded by a Lieutenant or a Sous-Lieutenant.

The number of battalions rose to ten in 1804 and then to eleven in 1805 to end up at the height of the Empire at fourteen, assembling more than 15,000 men. In wartime the battalions were doubled up, the new units thus created added "bis" to their number (e.g. 29bis).

The uniform was more or less established by the same decree of August 1801. In a convoy, together with the fore and aft drivers, ten NCOs and brigadiers (armed with a Light Cavalry sabre, a musketoon, and two pistols) were entrusted with protecting the guns. These horsemen rode remounts. The complete German-style harnessing was made up of four or six horses and in the first case comprised two fore harnesses and two rear harnesses.

The drivers' saddles, first of all bare, were given a half sheep's wool shabrack and a cover in 1805.

1805-1808

Shako Plate from the 4th Horse Artillery Regiment, in use in about 1806-1812, after Hilpert.

Brigadier from the Fourth Regiment wearing full dress in 1806, after Rousselot. The shako is decorated with a copper grenade with the number cut out.

Horse Artillery Gunner wearing full dress, in about 1806-1808, after the Zimmermann Manuscript. Note the absence of a shako plate and the presence of pockets on the long coat, as well as the rifle which was not officially issued to the Horse Artillery.

Horse Gunner wearing full dress in 1806, after Weiland.

Horse Gunner, in about 1806, after Bélanger. The shako plate seems to be a later model, with two crossed cannon surmounted by an eagle.

Maréchal-des-logis chef from the 1st Horse Artillery Regiment in 1806 after Noirmont and Marbot.

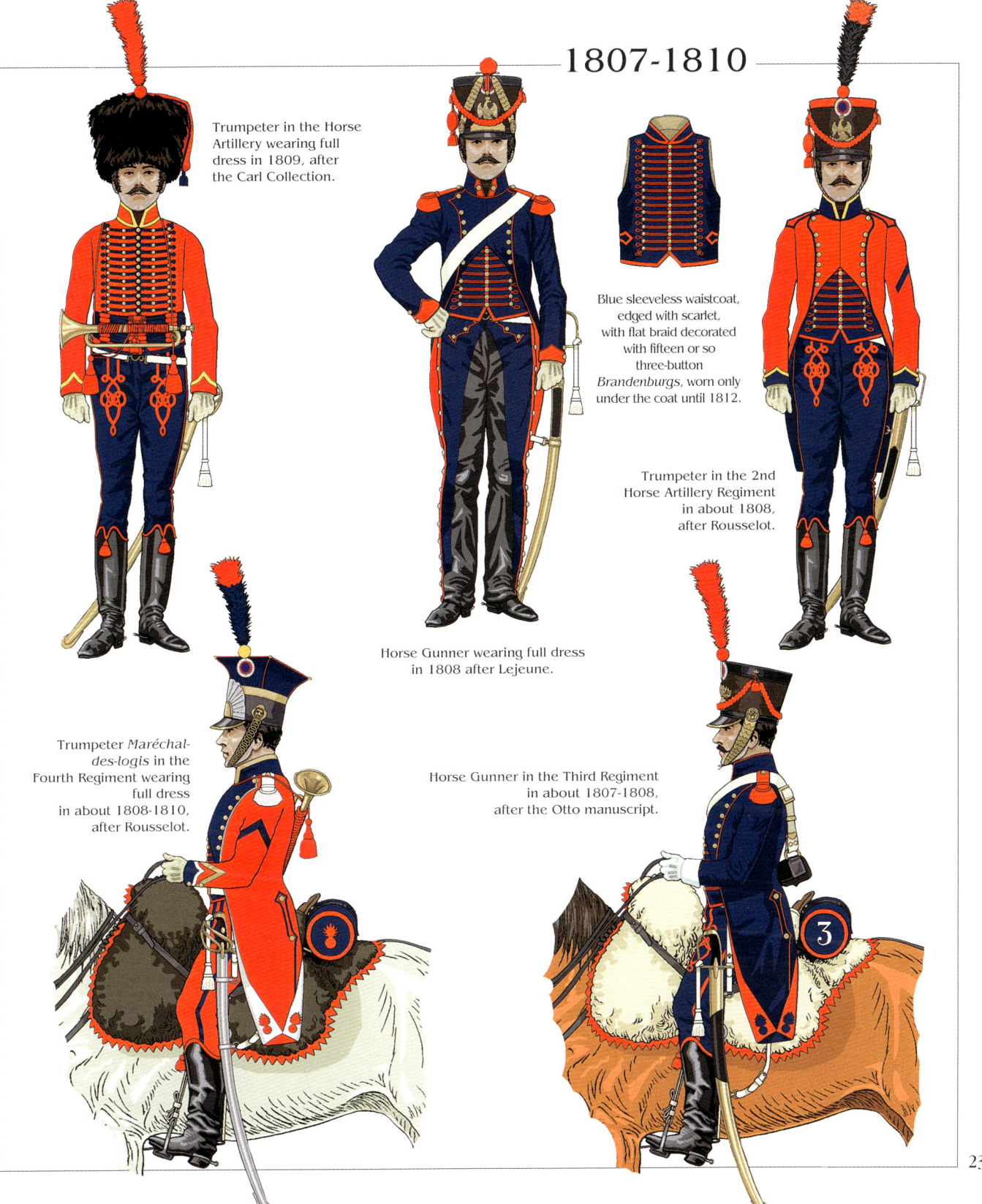

1809-1813

Gunner wearing campaign dress in 1809, after Berka. On the shako, the cockade has been positioned unusually, under a brass grenade.

Horse Gunner from *Prince d'Eckmühl*'s Army Corps in about 1810-1813 after the Hamburg Burgher. The rather strange, scaled epaulets clash with this rather austere uniform.

Horse Gunner from *Prince d'Eckmühl*'s Army Corps in about 1810-1813, after the Hamburg Burgher. This overcoat does not seem to have any pocket flaps on the turnbacks.

Gunner in the 4th Horse Artillery Regiment in 1809, after Suhr. Note the uniform's four-button facings and the yellow striping.

Horse Gunner wearing campaign dress in about 1809-1812, after Rousselot.

1809-1813

Light Artillery Officer from the Kingdom of Holland in 1807, according to the Hamburg Burgher.

When the Kingdom of Holland joined France the Dutch Artillery Corps, which had been reorganised on 26 December 1807, gained a 7th Horse Artillery Regiment and a 9th Foot Artillery Regiment. It comprised a headquarters, one foot Regiment with 3 seven-company battalions, four mounted companies of which one was a Guards Company, one five-company Workers battalion, one Pontoneer company, one Armourer company, one Miner company and one Train company.

Light Artillery Officer from the Kingdom of Holland wearing an overcoat in 1807, according to the Hamburg Burgher.

Trumpeter in the 2nd Light Artillery Company of the Kingdom of Holland in 1807, after the Hamburg Burgher.

Officer in the Light Artillery of the Kingdom of Holland in 1807, after the Hamburg Burgher.

Gunner from the 2nd Light Artillery Company of the Kingdom of Holland, wearing full dress in 1807, after the Hamburg Burgher.

1808-1813

Horse Artillery *Commandant* Picard in 1812, after a period portrait. From 1 January 1813 onwards, officers were forbidden from wearing the Hussar uniform.

Officer in the Horse Artillery wearing campaign dress in about 1808-1812, after Rousselot.

Officer in the *Prince d'Eckmühl*'s Army Corps wearing campaign dress in 1812, after the Hamburg Burgher.

Horse Artillery Lieutenant wearing regulation full dress in 1811, after Rousselot.

Horse Artillery Officer in about 1808-1810, after Rousselot.

1808-1813

Horse Artillery Officer wearing campaign dress in about 1809-1812, after Rousselot. On this character, the trousers are decorated with gold striping and the overcoat has a single epaulet.

Horse Artillery Officer wearing second uniform in about 1808-1812 (reconstitution).

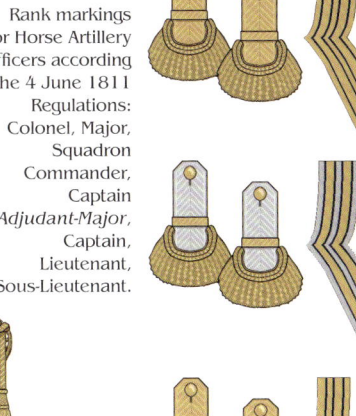

Rank markings for Horse Artillery officers according to the 4 June 1811 Regulations: Colonel, Major, Squadron Commander, Captain *Adjudant-Major*, Captain, Lieutenant, Sous-Lieutenant.

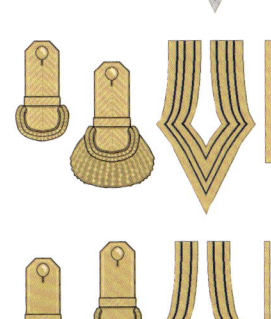

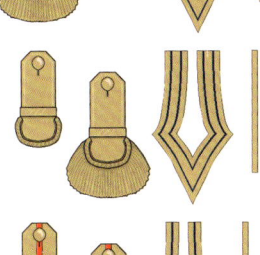

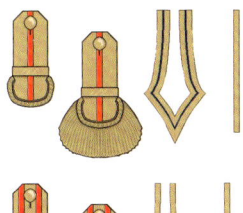

Horse Artillery Officer wearing full dress in about 1809-1812, after Rousselot. From 1 January 1813 onwards the colbacks were replaced once and for all by shakos.

Regulations appeared on 4 June 1811 covering the uniforms for all officers in the Imperial Artillery Corps in which there was a lot of fanciful dress. These very strict regulations specified which items were required for the uniforms and which were forbidden. In spite of this warning to the corps commanders, it wasn't before the end of the disastrous Russian Campaign that strict uniform regulations, the 1812 Bardin Regulations were applied.

Lieutenant wearing barracks dress, according to the 4 June 1811 regulations, comprising a forage cap and a waistcoat decorated with 18 rows of three buttons. The waistcoat and the cap had a 0.90 inch gold stripe for senior officers and a 0.55 inch one for junior ones.

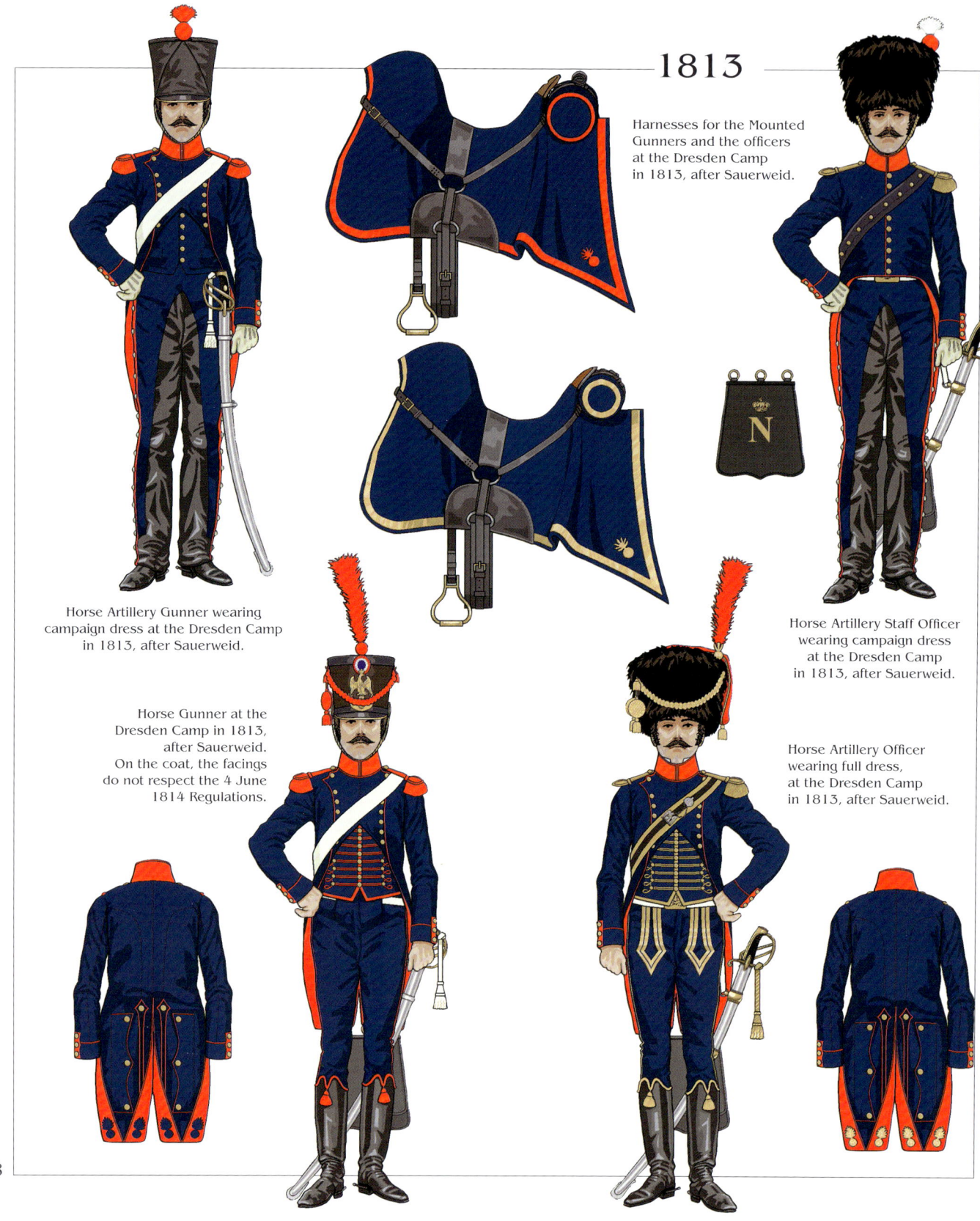

1808-1813

Horse Artillery Trumpeter in Spain, after El Guil.

Horse Artillery Regiment Staff Officer in Spain in 1813, after El Guil.

Horse Artillery Officer in marching dress in Spain, after El Guil.

Horse Gunner during the Spanish Campaign, after El Guil.

Horse Artillery Officer at Vittoria in 1813, after El Guil.

Horse Gunner in Spain, after El Guil.

1813-1815

7th Horse Artillery Regiment shako plate, like the Artillery model.

Horse Gunner's habit-veste with the three buttons on each facing, as stipulated by the 1812 Regulations.

Adjudant NCO from Headquarters of a Horse Artillery Regiment, according to the 1812 Regulations (reconstitution). The habit-veste has a scarlet epaulette and counter-epaulette with two gold lines, gold grenades on the turnbacks and two gold 15-year seniority chevrons. The shako has a scarlet stripe with a gold line and a white leather sabre-knot and gold and scarlet fringes.

Horse Gunner wearing campaign dress, according to the 1812 Regulations (reconstitution).

Gunner in the Horse Artillery in full dress in 1813, wearing breeches with scarlet trefoils, after Bucquoy.

Horse Gunner wearing a greatcoat which was also worn by officers, with a big collar, a cape with three buttons and sleeves, according to the 1812 Regulations, after Rousselot.

Horse Artillery Gunner wearing full dress, in about 1813-1814, according to the 1812 Regulations, after Rousselot.

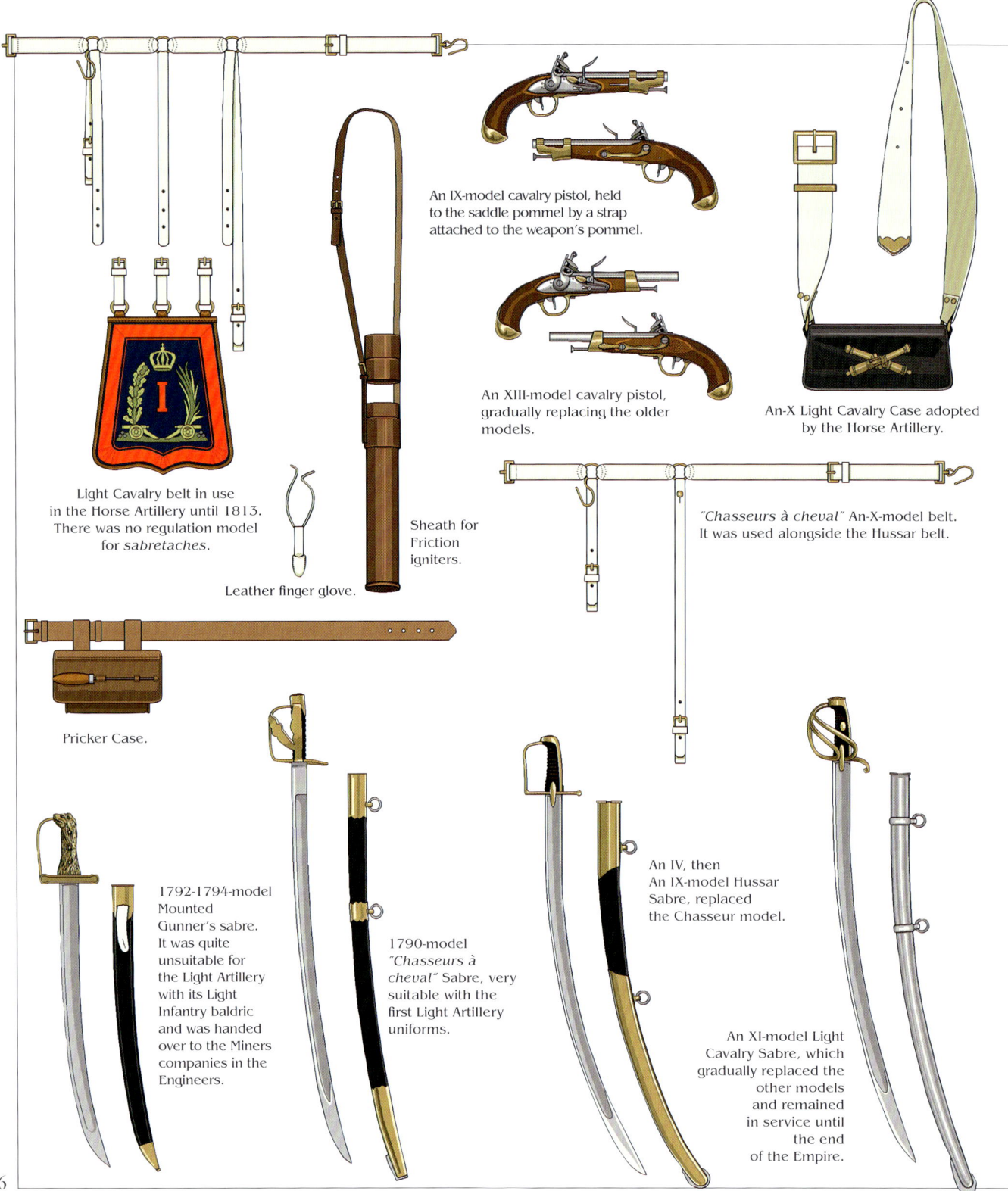

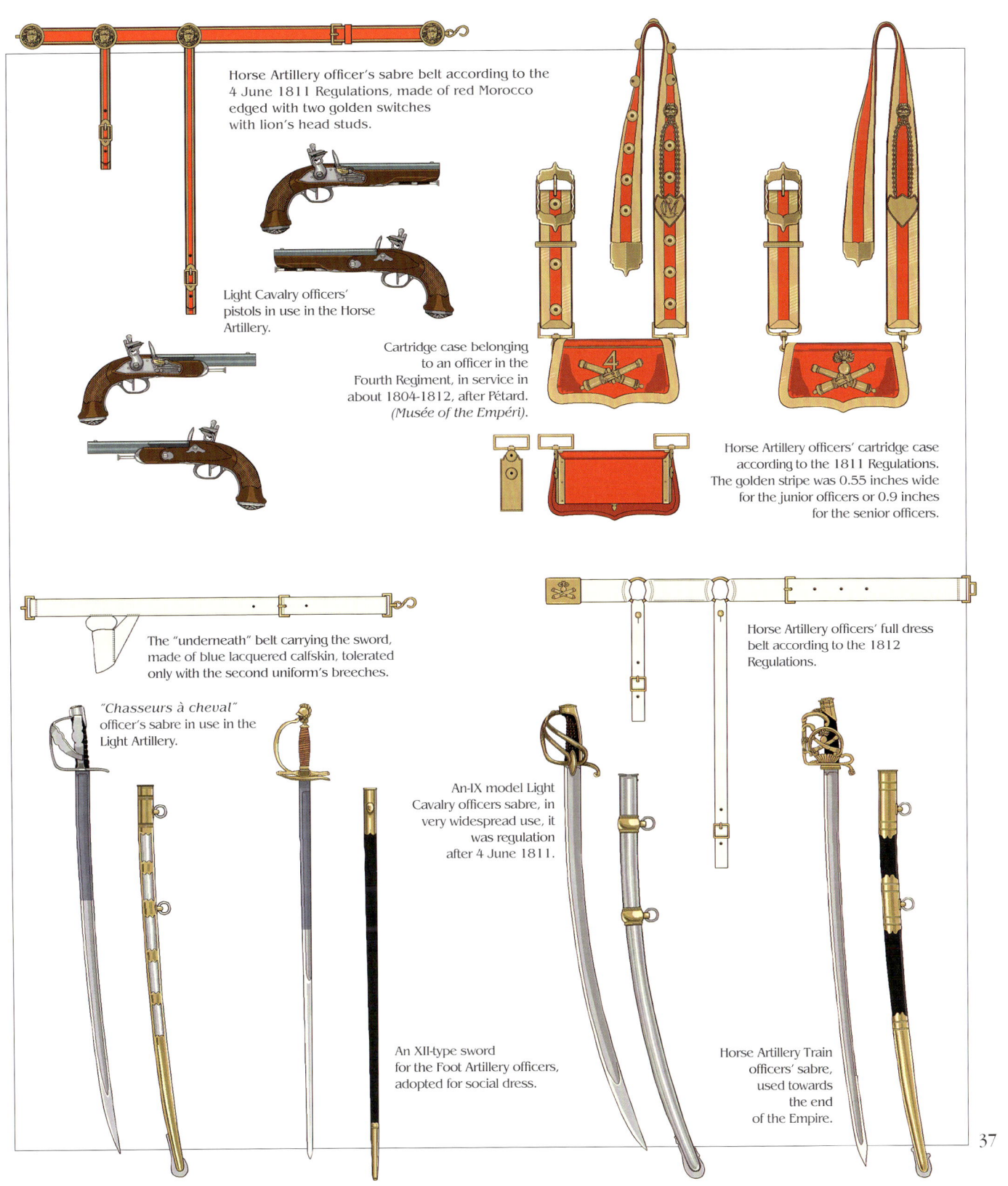

THE MOBILE ARTILLERY WURST

The Wurst system was borrowed off the Austrians and the Bavarians when the first Mobile (Horse) Artillery companies were formed in 1792.

In the following year, this caisson was tried out and twenty or so were built in the Douai arsenal and shared out, two per company. In the end, a light division consisted of four 8-pounders, two 14-inch howitzers supplied with fourteen Wurst caissons, each hitched to six or eight horses.

The Wurst caisson preserved the ammunition it was carrying better than the Gribeauval caisson because of the way the coffer had springs; its handling over all rough terrain was good, too. This system was only used in the vanguard alongside the cavalry.
In about 1792 it was planned to modify the 6-inch howitzers Wursts for the 12-lb guns.
This ever so-promising experiment turned out to be not very conclusive in the end, and was abandoned in 1795, in particular when one remembers that the Wurst had half the capacity of the Gribeauval and that it was structurally incompatible with other vehicles in service.

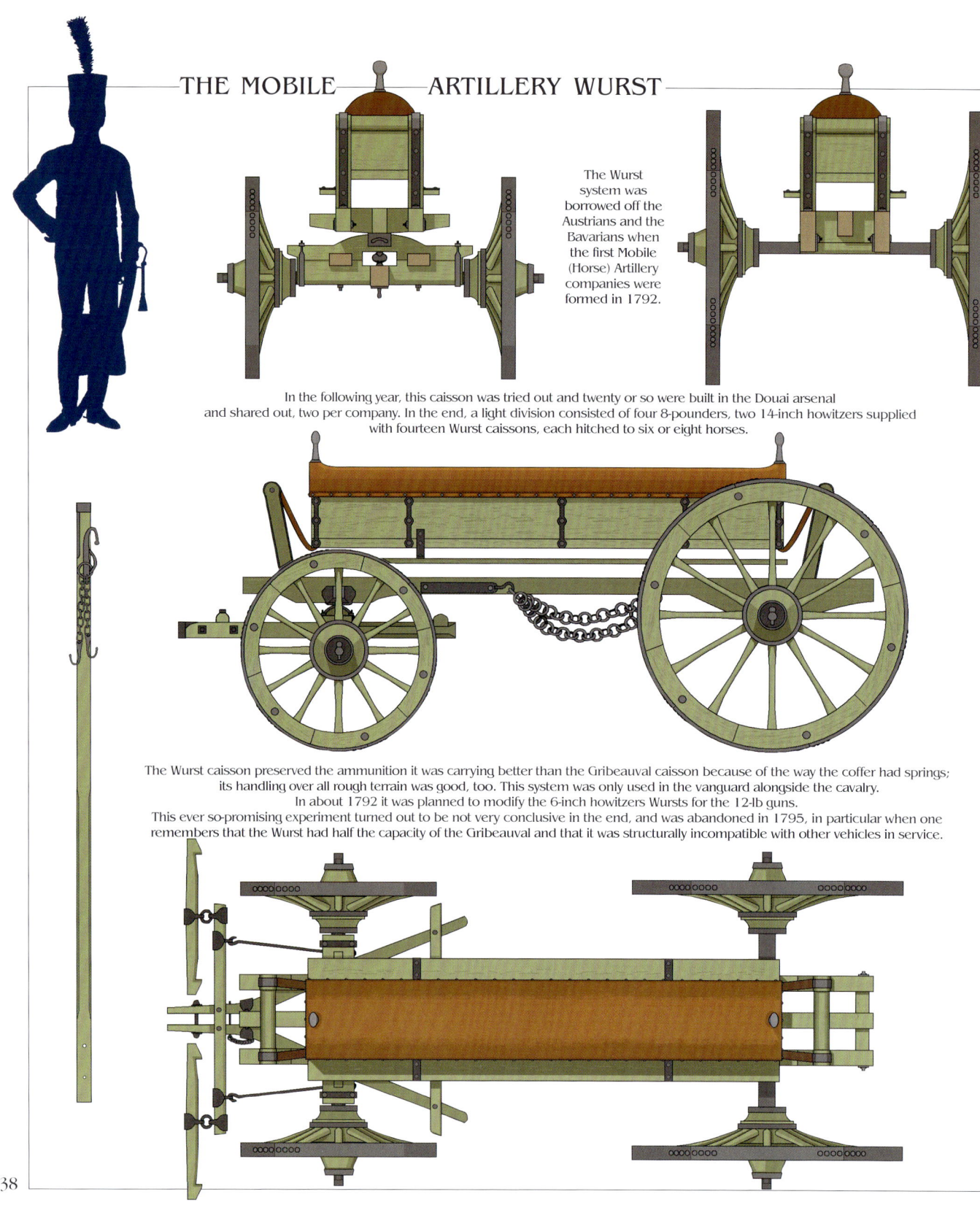

THE GRIBEAUVAL WAGON

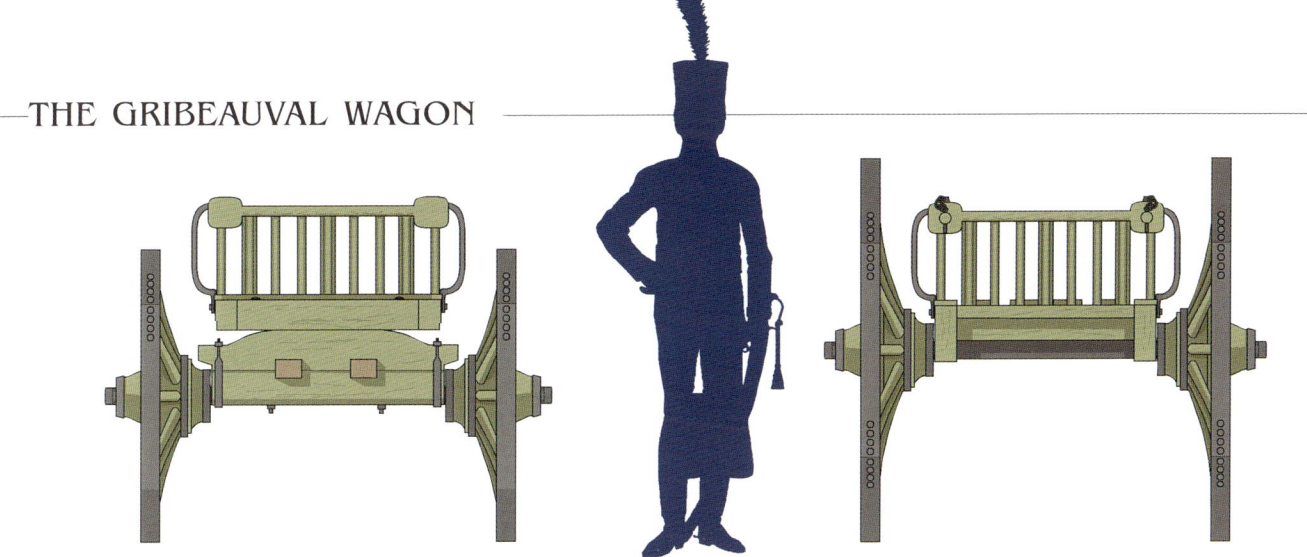

There were two or three wagons in each division of the Horse Artillery.

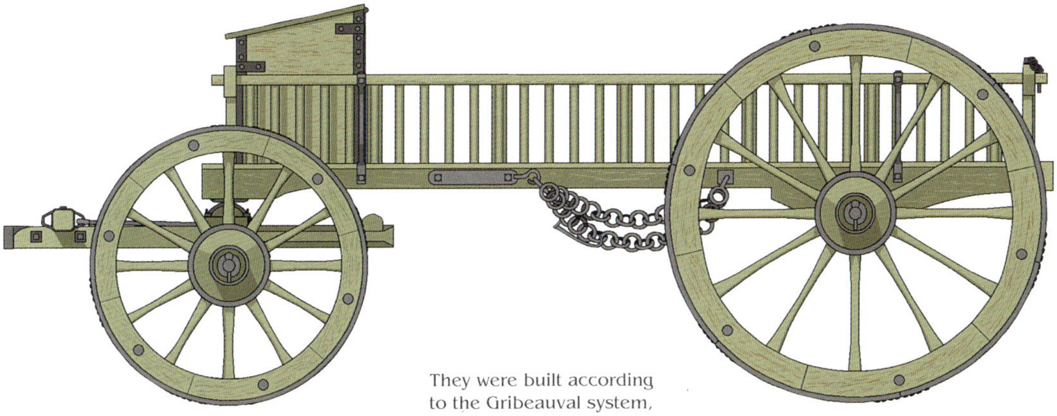

They were built according to the Gribeauval system, to carry 250 pioneer tools or five tons of powder, or spare parts for the divisional carriages, placed in the front coffer.

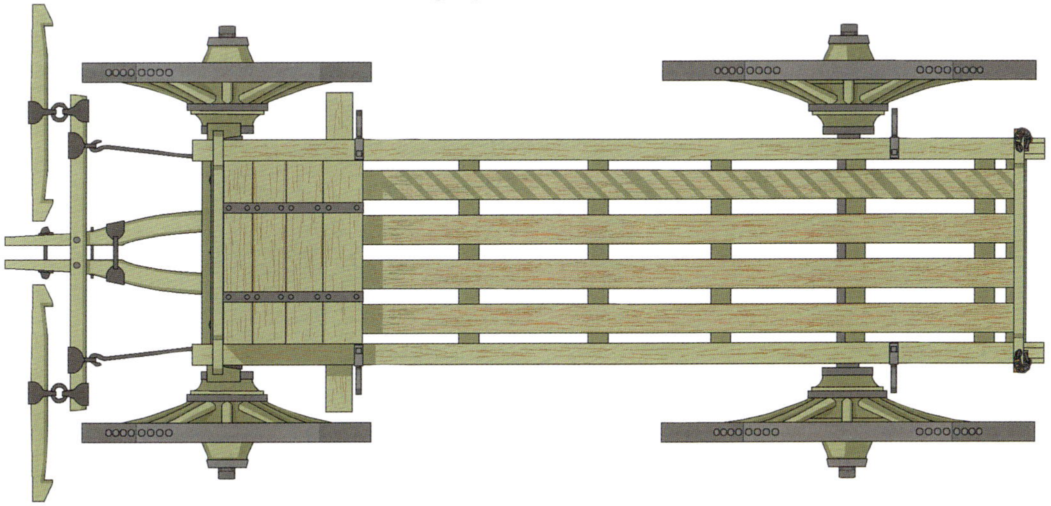

THE MOBILE ARTILLERY WURST

Supplying an 8-pounder when on campaign required two caissons, split into four big compartments lengthwise along the caisson, each split into three divisions. Each of these divisions was split into square sections. The 1st and the 4th compartments had 15 sections and the 2nd and 3rd had 18 sections containing 66 rounds, with the armament placed on top.
The Wurst 8-pounder caisson contained 60 cannonball cartridges, 6 ball cartridges, 6 bags of powder, 8 drag ropes, 3 bags of charge, 1 bag for quick-matches, 1 sheath of short shafts, 2 ordinary vent-prickers, 1 worm, 11 friction igniters, 90 quick-matches, 2 short shafts, 2 thumbstalls, 1 packet of fuses and 2 spatulas (after Gassendi).

The small coffer had to carry up to eight Gunners, thus saving on horses. The Wurst caisson had a rounded roof covered with leather and the seating was stuffed with horse hair for more comfort.

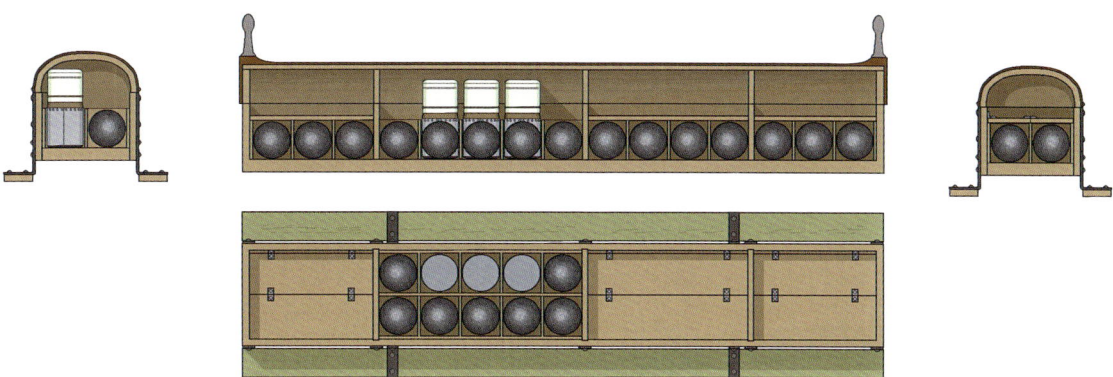

Supplying a 6-inch howitzer on campaign needed two caissons split into four big compartments separated in two sections lengthwise along the caisson. Each of these was divided into square sections. The 1st and 4th compartments had 6 sections, the 2nd 10 sections and the 3rd 8 sections, for thirty rounds, with the armament placed above it. The 1st, 3rd and 4th compartments were covered with shutters with the armament placed on top.
The Wurst howitzer caisson contained 27 shells, 3 ball cartridges, 30 bags for powder, 8 drag ropes, 3 bags for the charge, 1 bag for quick-matches, 1 short shafts sheath, 2 ordinary vent-prickers, 1 worm, 11 friction igniters, 40 quick-matches, 2 short shafts, 2 finger gloves, 1 packet of fuses, 2 spatulas, 2 pairs of bombardier cuffs, 1 one-pound powder measure, 1 quarter-pound measure, 4 *chasse-fusées*, 2 mallets, 1 quadrants and 250 splints (after Gassendi).

The Gunners kept their balance by holding on to each other and the pommels at both ends, and using two foot rests running the length of the caisson. Half Gunners faced forwards, the others faced backwards.

THE GRIBEAUVAL FORGE

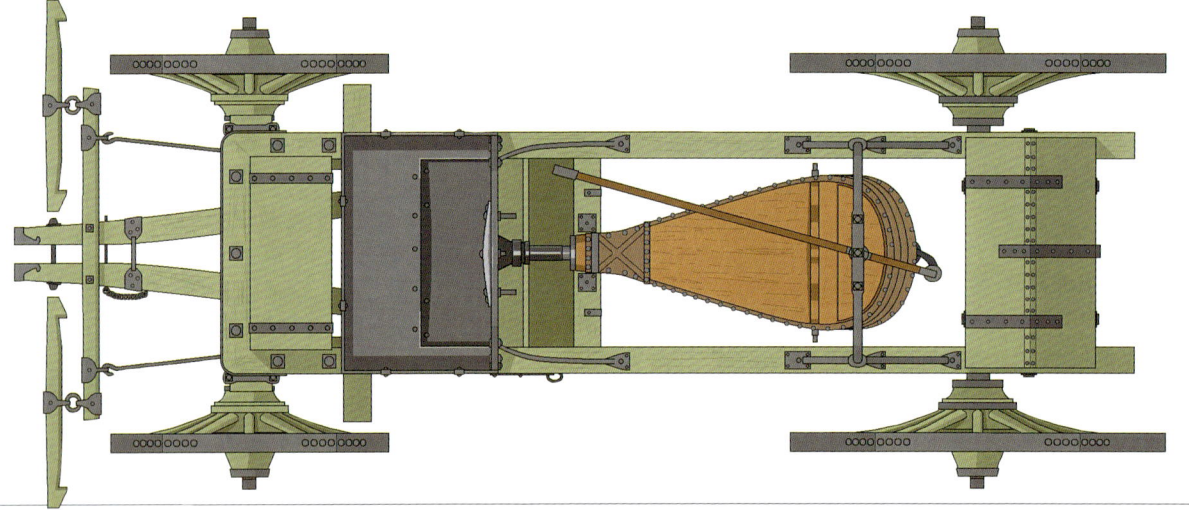

The so-called four-wheel mountain forge was in service from 1784 onwards and during the Empire, in all the *Grande Armée*'s corps. A second two wheel forge was used only in strongholds after that date. The artillery divisions formed required one forge for the battery and another for the train that accompanied it. The removable front coffer contained the artillery workers' tools and the rear one contained 55 pounds of coal. Limited numbers of a new forge were built in An-XI, using the same chassis as the caisson *(see Vol. 1, the Foot Artillery)*.

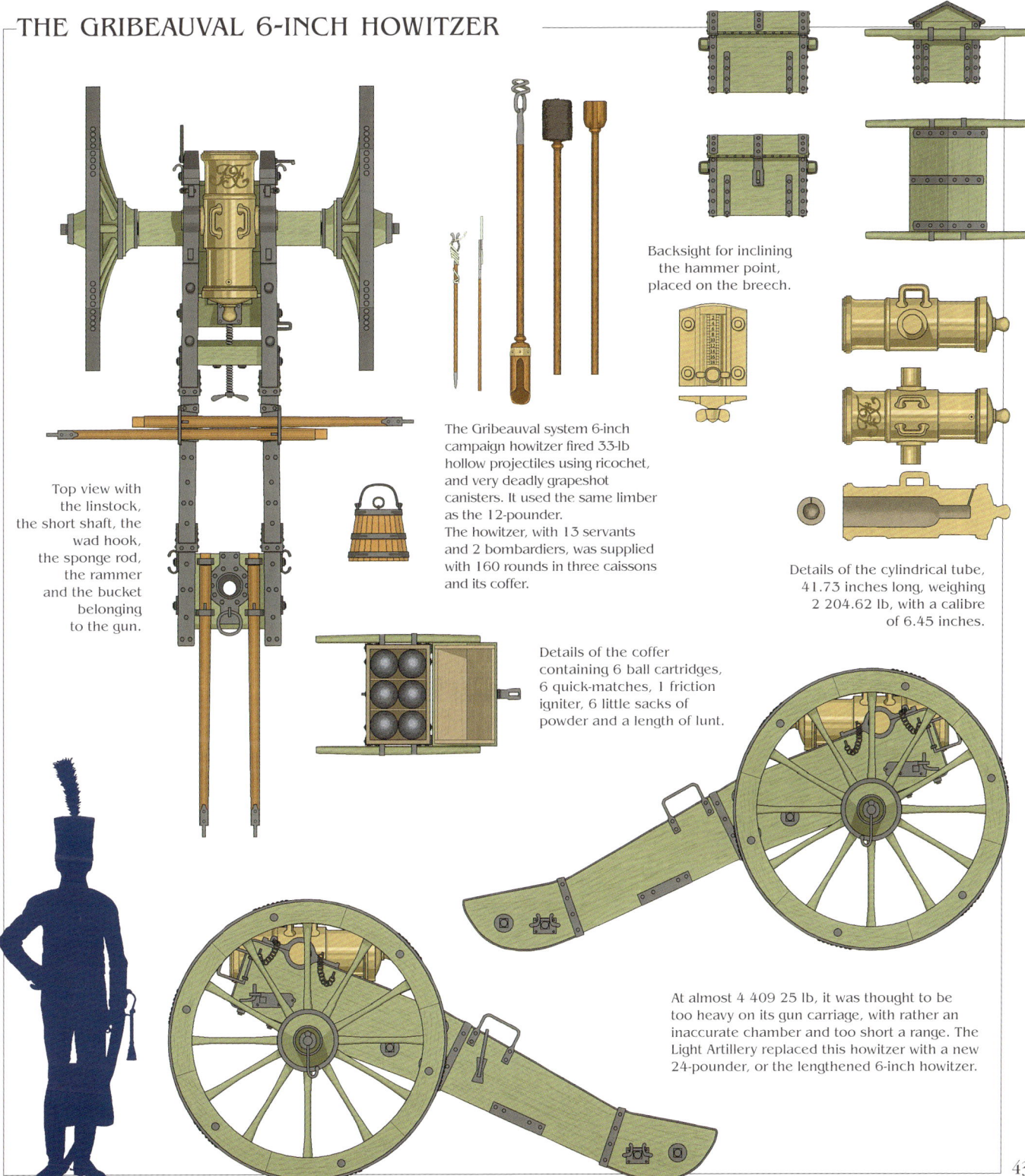

THE GRIBEAUVAL 8-POUND CANON

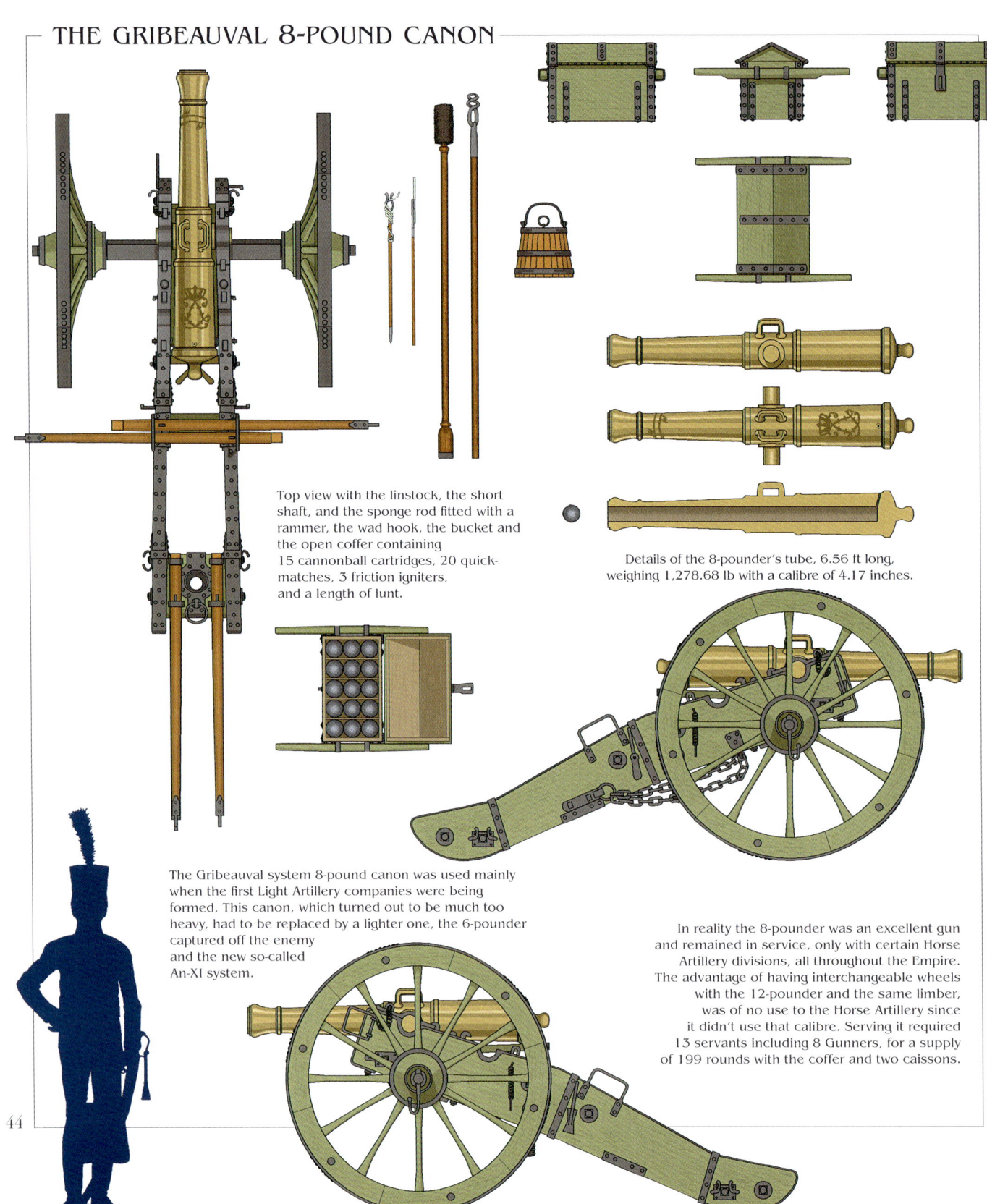

Top view with the linstock, the short shaft, and the sponge rod fitted with a rammer, the wad hook, the bucket and the open coffer containing 15 cannonball cartridges, 20 quick-matches, 3 friction igniters, and a length of lunt.

Details of the 8-pounder's tube, 6.56 ft long, weighing 1,278.68 lb with a calibre of 4.17 inches.

The Gribeauval system 8-pound canon was used mainly when the first Light Artillery companies were being formed. This canon, which turned out to be much too heavy, had to be replaced by a lighter one, the 6-pounder captured off the enemy and the new so-called An-XI system.

In reality the 8-pounder was an excellent gun and remained in service, only with certain Horse Artillery divisions, all throughout the Empire. The advantage of having interchangeable wheels with the 12-pounder and the same limber, was of no use to the Horse Artillery since it didn't use that calibre. Serving it required 13 servants including 8 Gunners, for a supply of 199 rounds with the coffer and two caissons.

THE GRIBEAUVAL 4-POUND CANON

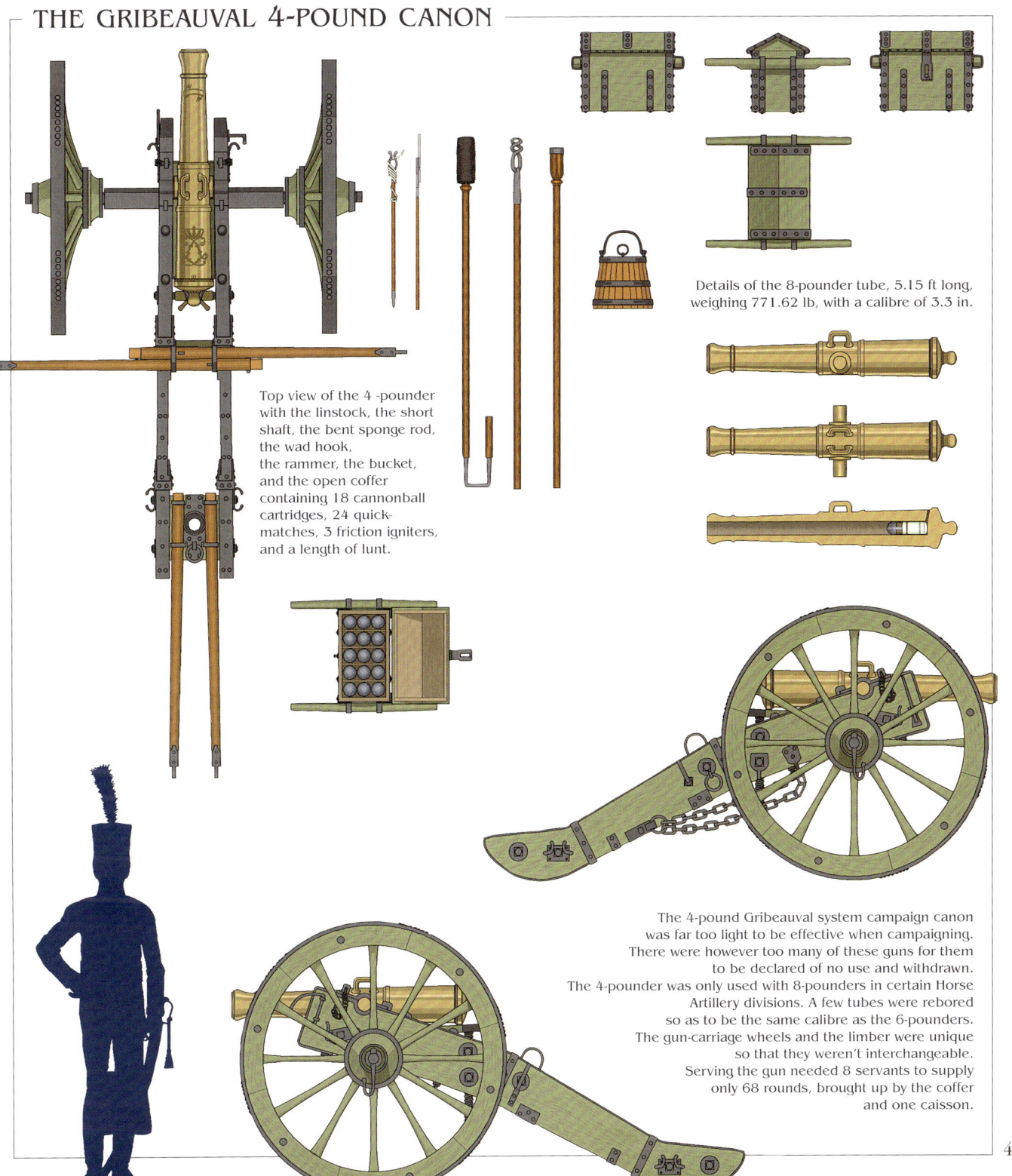

Top view of the 4-pounder with the linstock, the short shaft, the bent sponge rod, the wad hook, the rammer, the bucket, and the open coffer containing 18 cannonball cartridges, 24 quick-matches, 3 friction igniters, and a length of lunt.

Details of the 8-pounder tube, 5.15 ft long, weighing 771.62 lb, with a calibre of 3.3 in.

The 4-pound Gribeauval system campaign canon was far too light to be effective when campaigning. There were however too many of these guns for them to be declared of no use and withdrawn. The 4-pounder was only used with 8-pounders in certain Horse Artillery divisions. A few tubes were rebored so as to be the same calibre as the 6-pounders. The gun-carriage wheels and the limber were unique so that they weren't interchangeable. Serving the gun needed 8 servants to supply only 68 rounds, brought up by the coffer and one caisson.

45

THE GRIBEAUVAL SYSTEM LIMBER

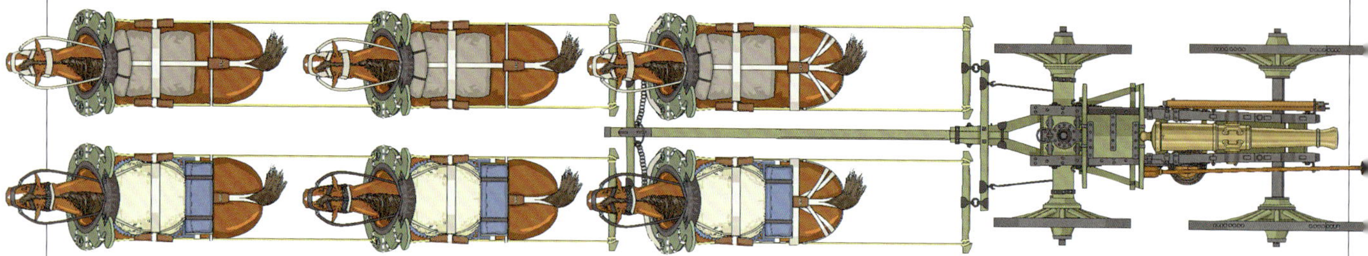

6-horse team for an 8-pound campaign gun seen from above.

Depending on the circumstances, the guns were hitched to 4- or 6-horse teams. The first two horses were hitched to the limber's wagon pole. The two or four leading horses were attached to the tip of the pole with whipple-trees.
The harnessed horses on the left were the carriers and were mounted by the drivers; whereas those on the right, the off-horses, were held by the drivers on the left using their right hands. The so-called German-style or French-style harnesses were made by cartage companies which were not under Artillery supervision. Here the canon is lying to the rear on its travelling trunnions.

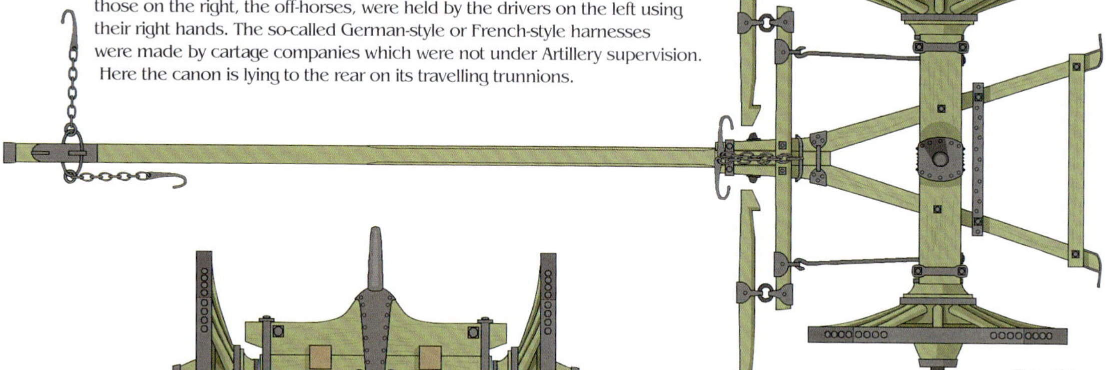

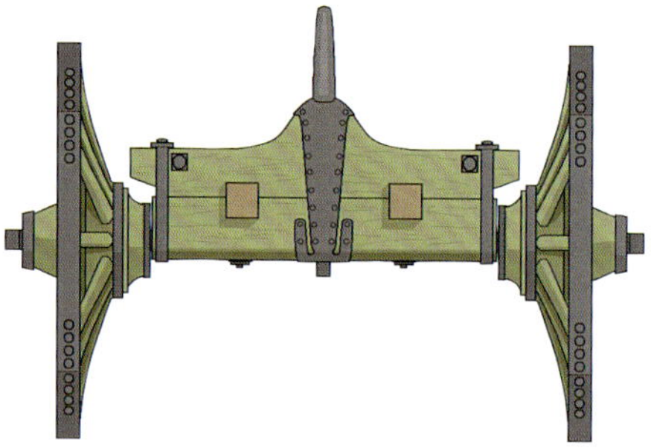

Top, side and rear views of the Gribeauval system limber for the 8- and 12-pounders and the 6-inch howitzer.

6-horse team for an 8-pound campaign gun seen from the left hand side.

GRIBEAUVAL SYSTEM ORDINARY CAISSON

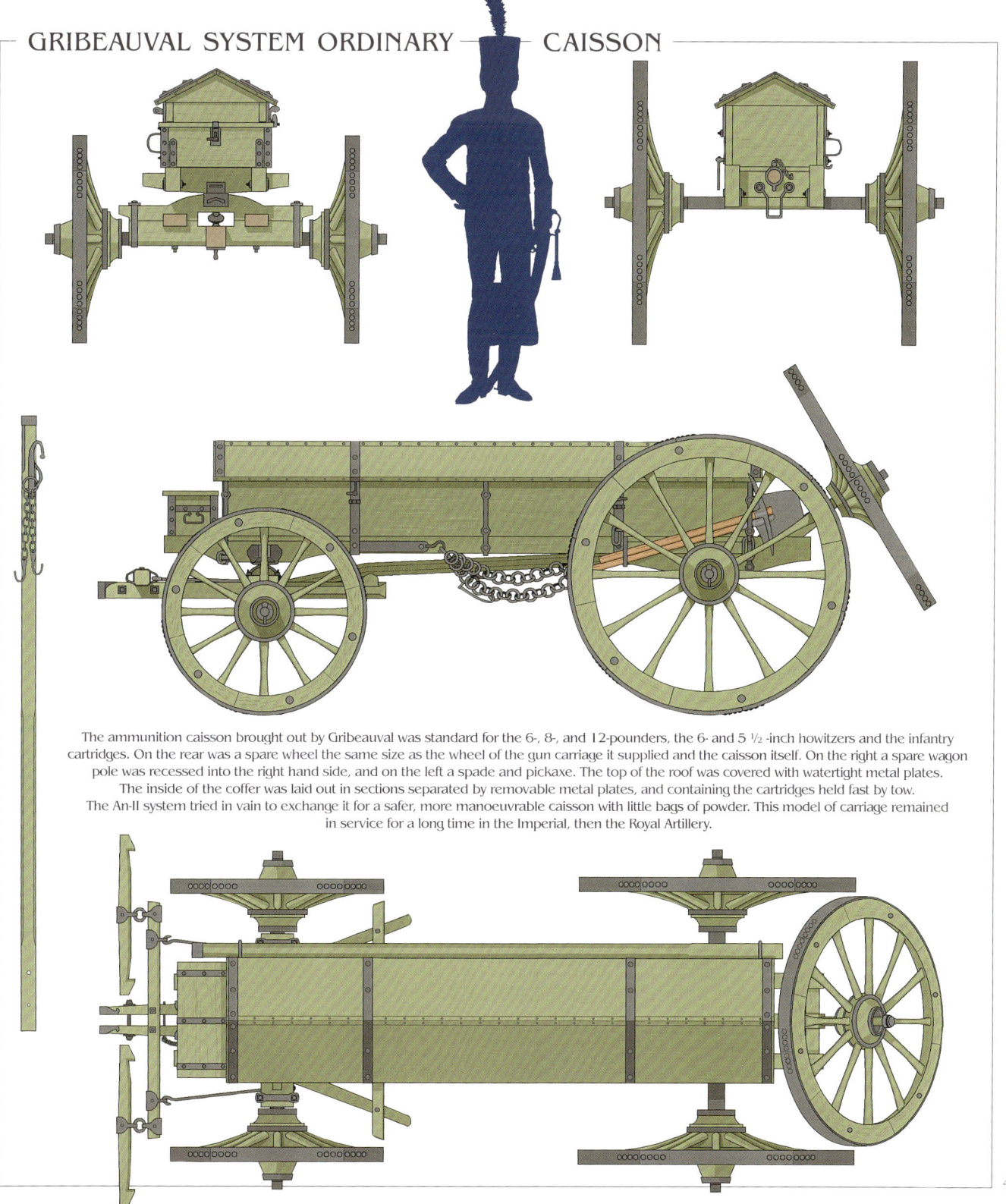

The ammunition caisson brought out by Gribeauval was standard for the 6-, 8-, and 12-pounders, the 6- and 5 ½-inch howitzers and the infantry cartridges. On the rear was a spare wheel the same size as the wheel of the gun carriage it supplied and the caisson itself. On the right a spare wagon pole was recessed into the right hand side, and on the left a spade and pickaxe. The top of the roof was covered with watertight metal plates. The inside of the coffer was laid out in sections separated by removable metal plates, and containing the cartridges held fast by tow. The An-II system tried in vain to exchange it for a safer, more manoeuvrable caisson with little bags of powder. This model of carriage remained in service for a long time in the Imperial, then the Royal Artillery.

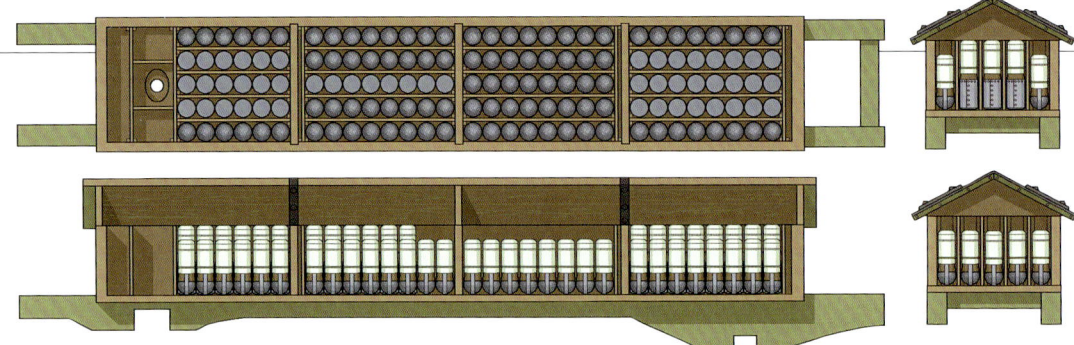

The disposition for the 4-pounder in service in the Horse Artillery in some of the batteries (one caisson per gun) contained 2 bags for the charge, 1 bag for quick-matches, 1 sheath for friction igniters, 2 ordinary vent-prickers, 2 worms, 2 short shafts, 2 thumb stalls, 2 spatula pour stuffing, all placed in the first section. The other sections contained 100 cannonball cartridges with their sabots, 26 large ball cartridges, 24 little ball cartridges, 200 quick-matches, 25 friction igniters, 20 little bags of powder, 12 length of lunt and 6 drag ropes.

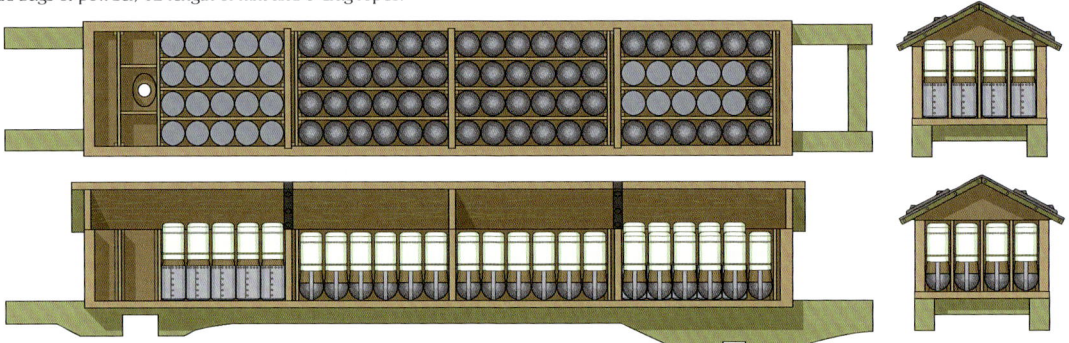

The layout for a- 8 -pounder (two caissons per gun) consisted of 4 compartments of 4 sections lengthwise, with 3 bags for the charge, 1 bag for quick-matches, 1 sheath for friction igniters, 2 short shafts, 2 ordinary vent-prickers, 1 worm, 2 thumb stalls, 2 spatulas for stuffing, placed in the forward section. To this must be added 3 bags for the charge, 3 drag ropes in both caissons. The other sections held 62 cannonballs cartridges with their sabots, 10 large ball cartridges, 20 little ball cartridges, 122 quick-matches, 16 friction igniters, 12 lengths of fuse, 30 little bags of powder and 8 drag ropes.

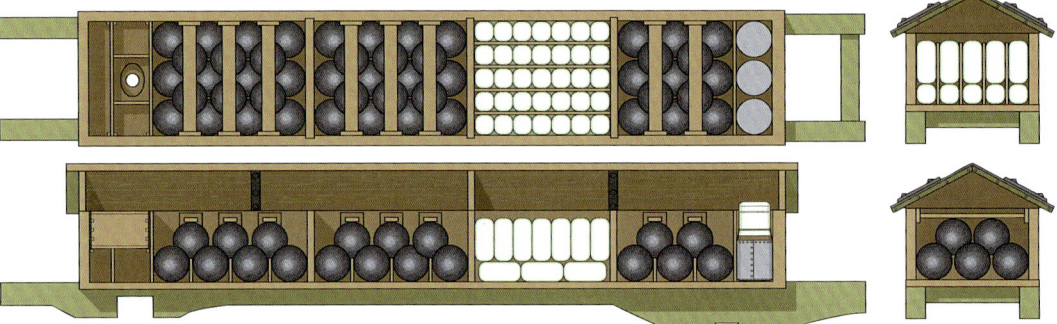

The layout for a 6-inch howitzer (three caissons per howitzer) contained 49 shells, 3 ball cartridges, 70 quick-matches, 9 friction igniters, 52 little bags of powder, 12 lengths of fuse, 1 bag for friction igniters, 1 ordinary priming wire, 1 worm, 2 thumb stalls, 2 short shafts, 3 bags for charge, 2 mallets, 1 *tire-fusée*, 1 funnel, 1 one-pound measure, 1 quarter pound measure, 4 *chasse-fusées*, 200 splints, 2 pairs of bombardier cuffs, 2 spatula for stuffing the tow and 10 drag ropes spread out in the caissons.

Team for an artillery caisson, seen from the left.

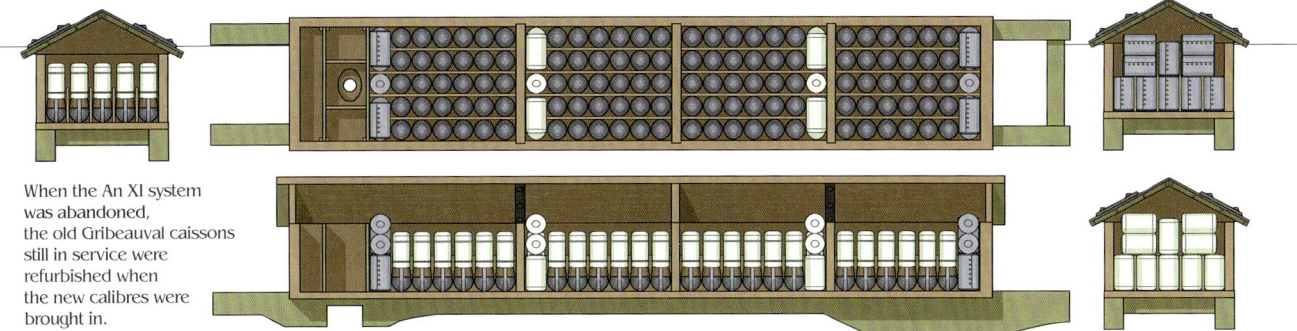

When the An XI system was abandoned, the old Gribeauval caissons still in service were refurbished when the new calibres were brought in.

The layout for the new 6-pounder (one caisson per gun) enabled it to contain 120 cannonballs cartridges with sabots, 10 large ball cartridges, 10 small ball cartridges with 20 little bags for powder, 190 quick-matches, 24 friction igniters, 12 lengths of fuse, 2 ordinary vent-prickers, 2 vent-prickers with a worm, 2 thumb stalls, 4 drag ropes, 2 bags for the charge, 1 bag for quick-matches, 1 sheath for friction igniters, 2 short shafts, 2 spatula pour stuffing the great quantity of tow.

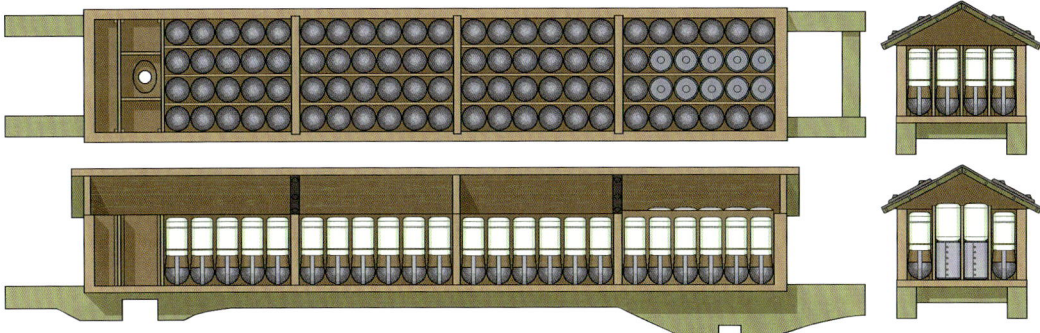

The layout for one 8-pounder (two caissons per gun) now contained 82 cannonballs cartridges with sabots, 5 cartridges for big balls, 5 cartridges for little balls, 10 little sacks of powder, 122 quick-matches, 16 friction igniters, 12 lengths of fuse, 8 drag ropes, 3 bags for the charge, 1 bag for quick-matches, 1 sheath for friction igniters, 2 short shafts, 2 ordinary vent-prickers, 1 worm, 2 finger gloves, 2 spatula for stuffing the tow. Three further bags for the charge, or three other drag ropes in both caissons.

The layout for the new 5 ½-inch Howitzer (two caissons per howitzer) contained 72 shells, 3 boxes for balls and 75 little sacks of powder, 100 quick-matches, 4 friction igniters, 12 lengths of fuse, 1 ordinary priming wire, 1 worm, 2 short shafts, 2 finger gloves, 1 funnel, 1 one-pound measure, 1 quarter-pound measure, 2 mallets, 1 *tire-fusée*, 200 splints, 2 pairs of bombardier cuffs, 2 spatulas for stuffing the tow and in the two caissons: 9 friction igniters, 4 *chasse-fusées*, 8 drag ropes, 3 bags for the charge, 1 bag for quick-matches and 1 sheath for friction igniters.

The same four horse team seen from above.

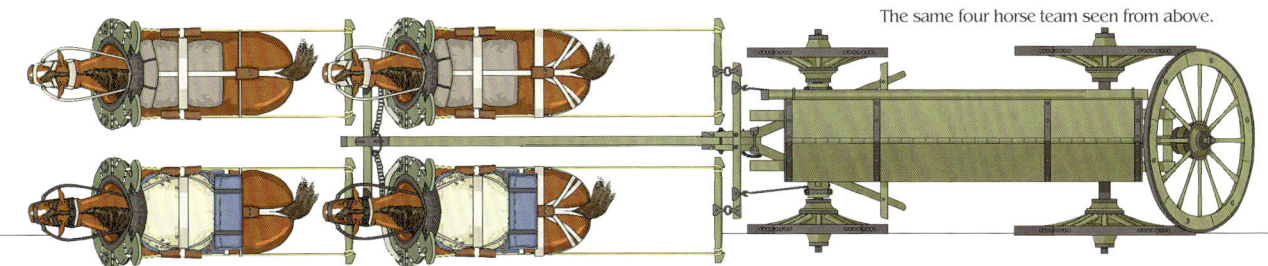

THE 1795-MODEL 6-INCH LONG RANGE HOWITZER

Coffer containing 6 little sacks and cannonballs, the wad hook, the sponge rod, the rammer, the linstock, the short shaft, the bucket, to which had to be added the pointing levers, drag ropes, ammunition bags, sheathes for lances, bags for quick-matches, priming wire and finger gloves.

1795-model 6-inch long range Howitzer, on an An-XI gun-carriage.

The first improvement that was made to the Gribeauval system in 1795 was lengthening the tube of the 6-inch howitzer to increase its range and its accuracy compared with the Prussian model. This gun was intended only for the Foot Artillery with the 12-pounder canon, on which the Gribeauval or An-XI gun carriages were interchangeable.

THE AN XI SYSTEM 24-POUND HOWITZER

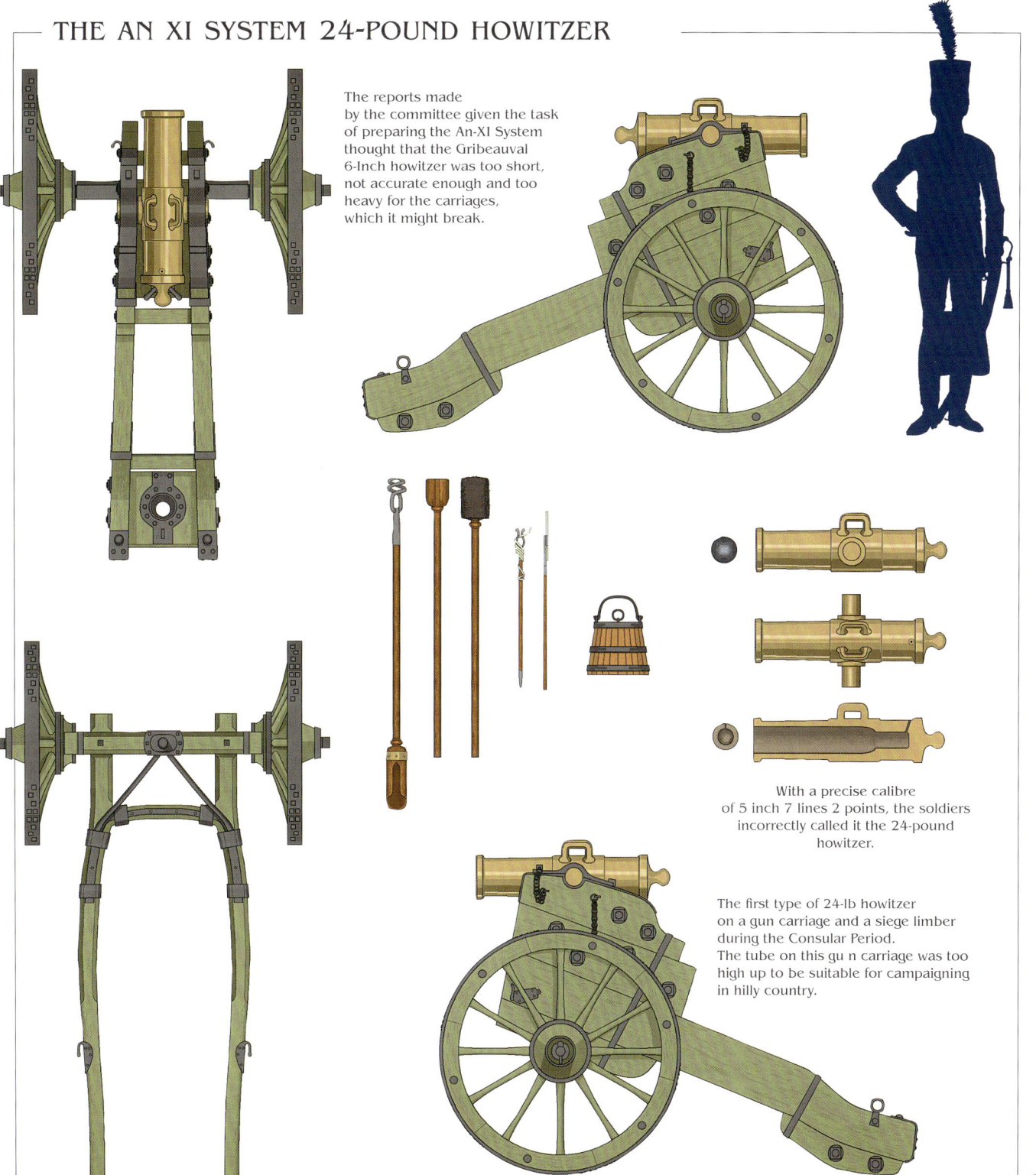

The reports made by the committee given the task of preparing the An-XI System thought that the Gribeauval 6-Inch howitzer was too short, not accurate enough and too heavy for the carriages, which it might break.

With a precise calibre of 5 inch 7 lines 2 points, the soldiers incorrectly called it the 24-pound howitzer.

The first type of 24-lb howitzer on a gun carriage and a siege limber during the Consular Period. The tube on this gun carriage was too high up to be suitable for campaigning in hilly country.

THE AN XI SYSTEM 24-POUND HOWITZER

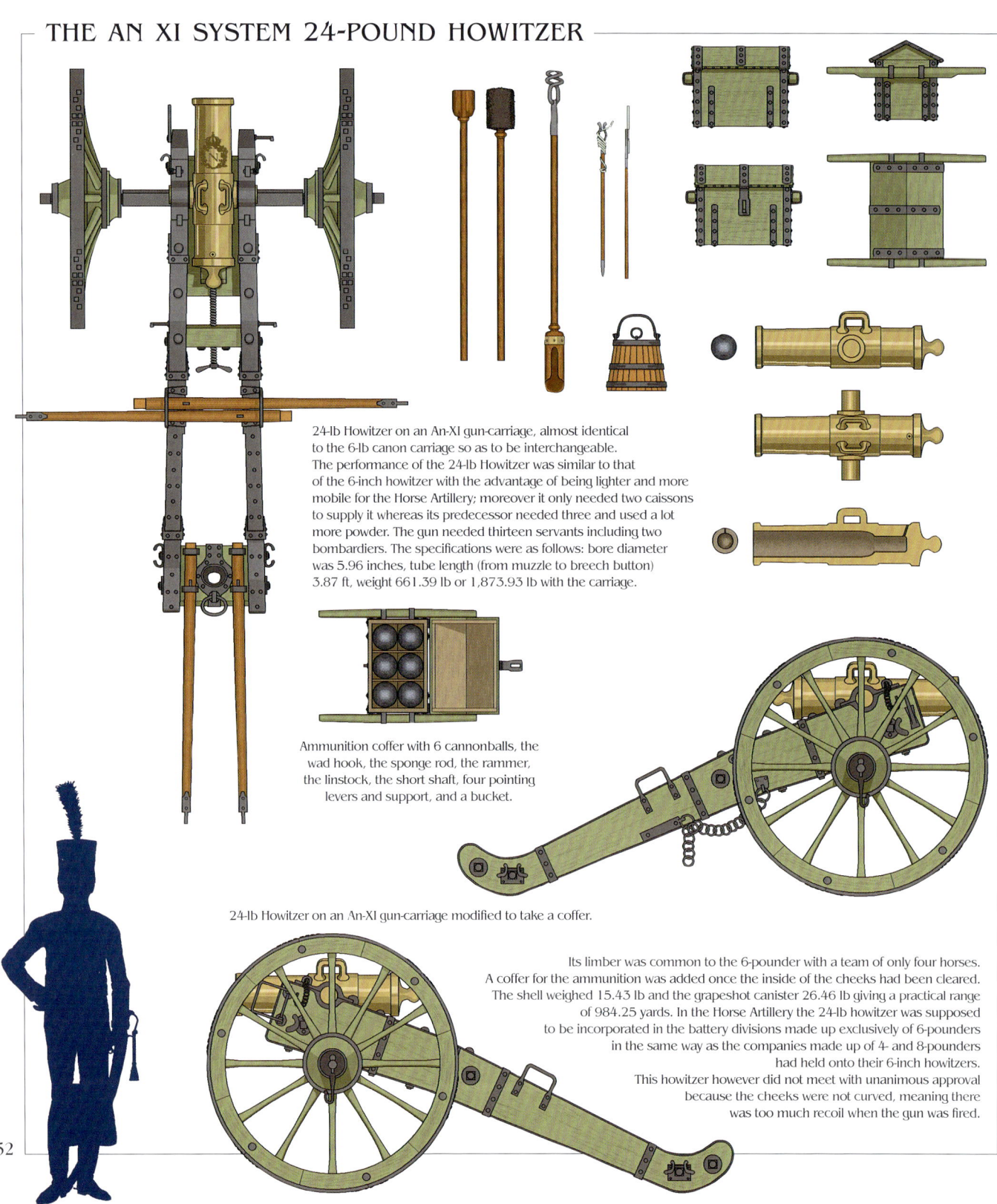

24-lb Howitzer on an An-XI gun-carriage, almost identical to the 6-lb canon carriage so as to be interchangeable. The performance of the 24-lb Howitzer was similar to that of the 6-inch howitzer with the advantage of being lighter and more mobile for the Horse Artillery; moreover it only needed two caissons to supply it whereas its predecessor needed three and used a lot more powder. The gun needed thirteen servants including two bombardiers. The specifications were as follows: bore diameter was 5.96 inches, tube length (from muzzle to breech button) 3.87 ft, weight 661.39 lb or 1,873.93 lb with the carriage.

Ammunition coffer with 6 cannonballs, the wad hook, the sponge rod, the rammer, the linstock, the short shaft, four pointing levers and support, and a bucket.

24-lb Howitzer on an An-XI gun-carriage modified to take a coffer.

Its limber was common to the 6-pounder with a team of only four horses. A coffer for the ammunition was added once the inside of the cheeks had been cleared. The shell weighed 15.43 lb and the grapeshot canister 26.46 lb giving a practical range of 984.25 yards. In the Horse Artillery the 24-lb howitzer was supposed to be incorporated in the battery divisions made up exclusively of 6-pounders in the same way as the companies made up of 4- and 8-pounders had held onto their 6-inch howitzers. This howitzer however did not meet with unanimous approval because the cheeks were not curved, meaning there was too much recoil when the gun was fired.

THE AN-XI SYSTEM 6-POUNDER

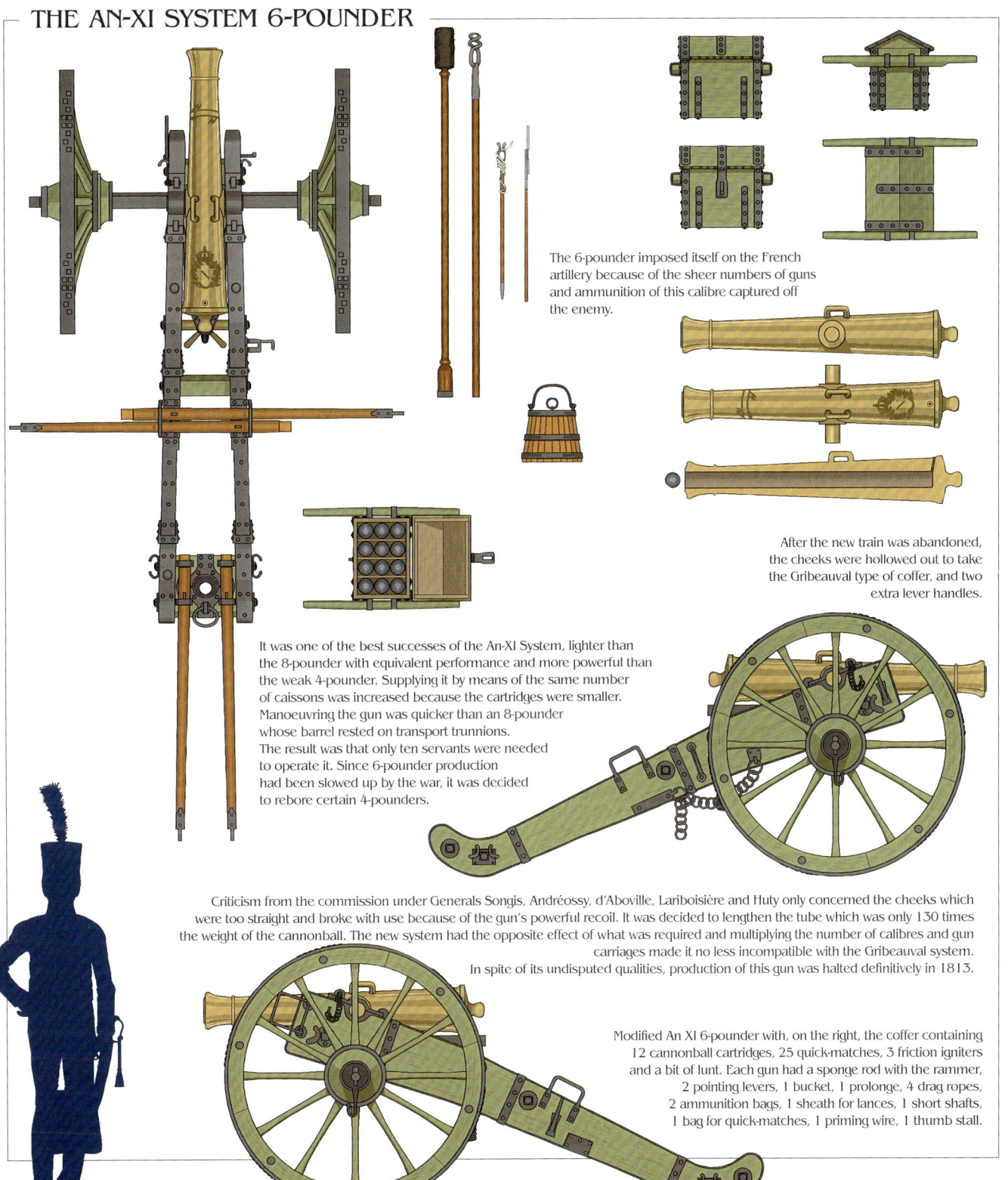

The 6-pounder imposed itself on the French artillery because of the sheer numbers of guns and ammunition of this calibre captured off the enemy.

It was one of the best successes of the An-XI System, lighter than the 8-pounder with equivalent performance and more powerful than the weak 4-pounder. Supplying it by means of the same number of caissons was increased because the cartridges were smaller. Manoeuvring the gun was quicker than an 8-pounder whose barrel rested on transport trunnions. The result was that only ten servants were needed to operate it. Since 6-pounder production had been slowed up by the war, it was decided to rebore certain 4-pounders.

After the new train was abandoned, the cheeks were hollowed out to take the Gribeauval type of coffer, and two extra lever handles.

Criticism from the commission under Generals Songis, Andréossy, d'Aboville, Lariboisière and Huty only concerned the cheeks which were too straight and broke with use because of the gun's powerful recoil. It was decided to lengthen the tube which was only 130 times the weight of the cannonball. The new system had the opposite effect of what was required and multiplying the number of calibres and gun carriages made it no less incompatible with the Gribeauval system. In spite of its undisputed qualities, production of this gun was halted definitively in 1813.

Modified An XI 6-pounder with, on the right, the coffer containing 12 cannonball cartridges, 25 quick-matches, 3 friction igniters and a bit of lunt. Each gun had a sponge rod with the rammer, 2 pointing levers, 1 bucket, 1 prolonge, 4 drag ropes, 2 ammunition bags, 1 sheath for lances, 1 short shafts, 1 bag for quick-matches, 1 priming wire, 1 thumb stall.

THE AN-XI SYSTEM LIMBER

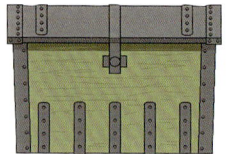

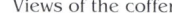
Views of the coffer.

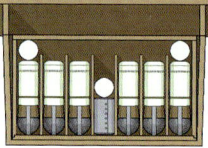
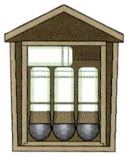

Cross sections of the coffer
and of the chest with the layout
for the 6-pound cartridges.

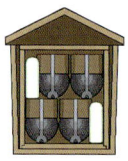

Cross section of the coffer and of the chest
with the layout for the 24-pound shells.

The limber with an immediate supply coffer was a modern and ambitious part of the new system which wanted to replace the coffer recessed between the gun-carriage cheeks.
After it was put into service, the new model was abandoned in favour of the old version because of the serious risk of accidents.

Only the Horse Artillery continued to use this equipment to draw the new 6- and 24-pound guns, whose cheeks had not been adapted for the coffers. According to the same principle that was used for the big ammunition caissons the coffer had to hold a removable chest containing the cartridges.

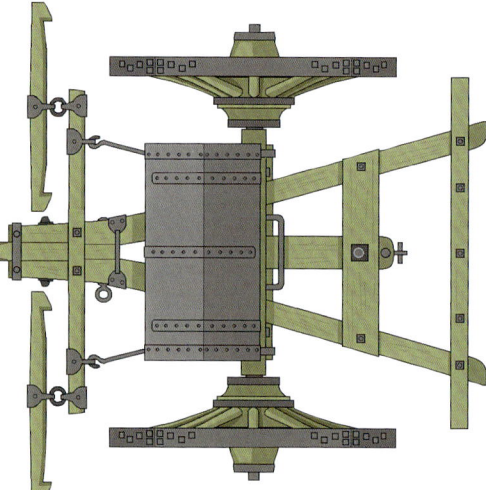

Top view of the limber.

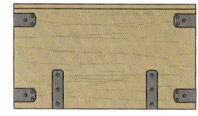

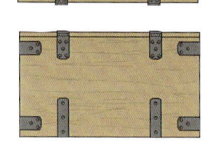

Views of the chest.

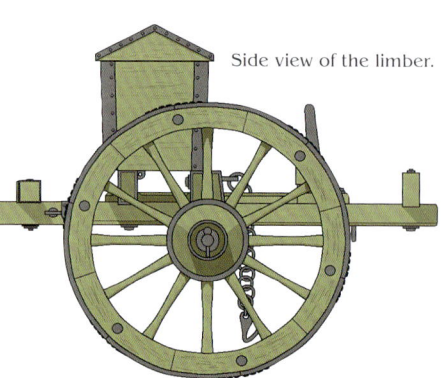

Side view of the limber.

THE AN-XI SYSTEM CAISSON

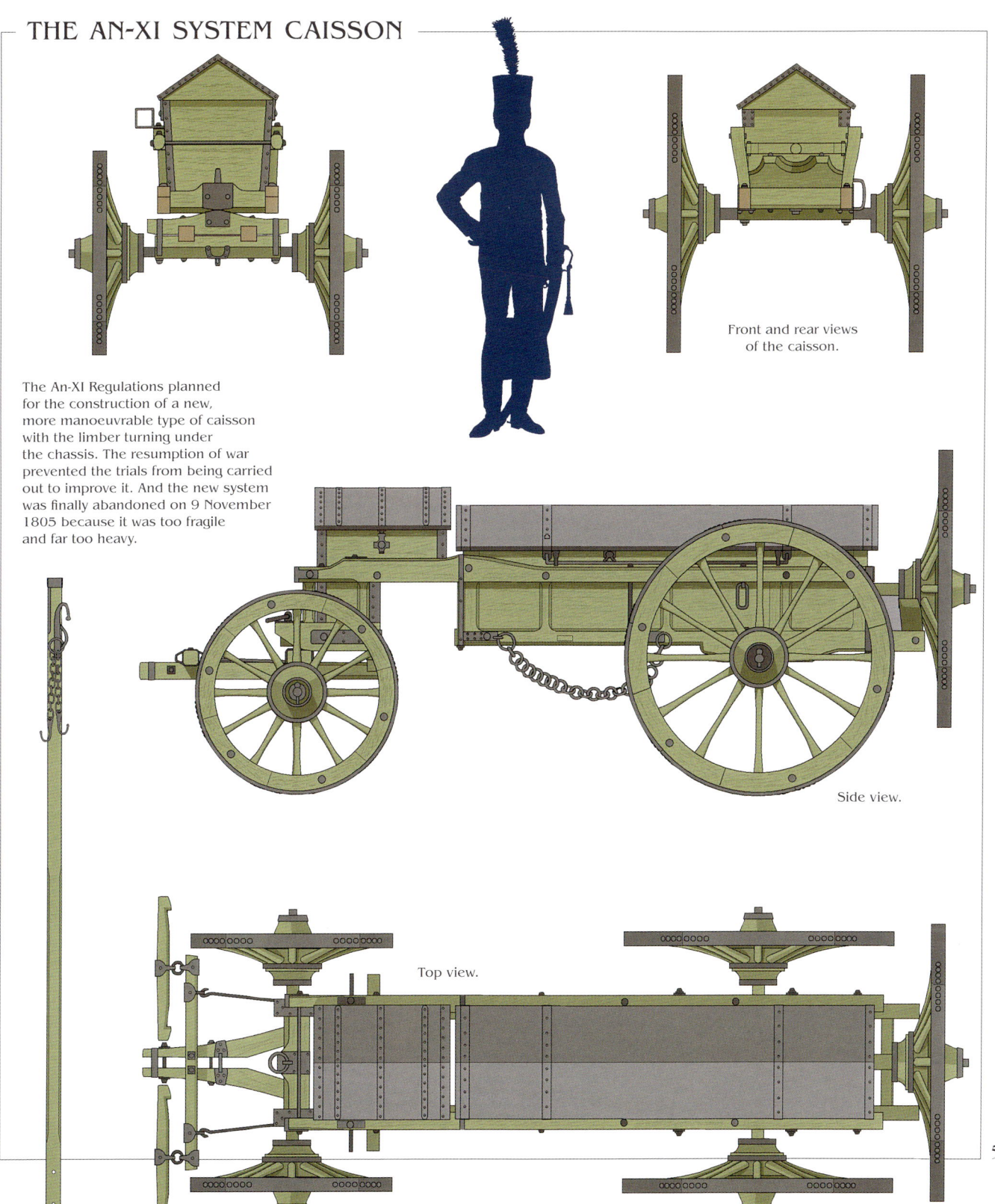

Front and rear views of the caisson.

The An-XI Regulations planned for the construction of a new, more manoeuvrable type of caisson with the limber turning under the chassis. The resumption of war prevented the trials from being carried out to improve it. And the new system was finally abandoned on 9 November 1805 because it was too fragile and far too heavy.

Side view.

Top view.

THE AN-XI SYSTEM CAISSON

The layout for the 5 ½ inch campaign howitzer (three caissons per howitzer) comprising 10 chests for shells with their sabots, 1 chest of ball cartridges in the main coffer and two chests of shells with their sabots in the front coffer. All the chests together contained 72 shells, 72 little bags of powder and 4 ball boxes with 4 little bags of powder. Spread out over this collection were 1 bag for the charge, 1 bag for quick-matches, 100 quick-matches, 4 friction igniters, 12 lengths of fuse, 1 ordinary priming wire, 1 worm, 2 short shafts, 2 finger gloves, 1 funnel, 1 quarter pound powder measure, 1 one pound powder measure, 2 mallets, 1 *tire-fusée*, 200 splints, 2 pairs of bombardier cuffs and 2 spatulas for stuffing the oakum. Also to be added: 1 sheath for friction igniters, 9 friction igniters, 4 *chasse-fusées*, 8 drag ropes, shared out in the three caissons.

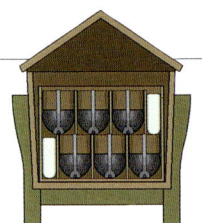
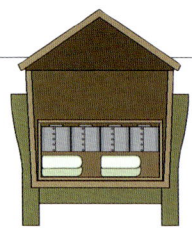
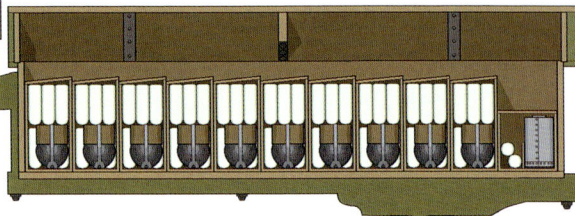
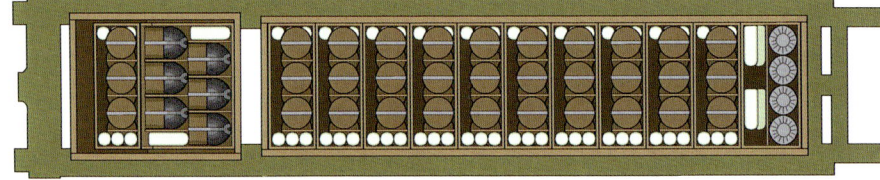
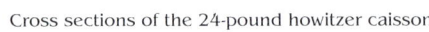

Cross sections of the 24-pound howitzer caisson.

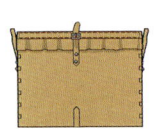

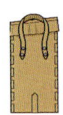

Cross section of the watertight chests for the shells and the ball boxes for the 24-pound howitzer.

Lay out for the 6-pounder (one caisson per gun) comprising 9 chests of cannonballs cartridges and 2 chests of ball cartridges in the main coffer, 2 chests of extra cannonballs cartridges the front coffer. The set of watertight chests contained 132 cannonballs cartridges with sabots, 12 boxes for big balls, 12 boxes for little balls, 24 little sacks of powder. In each chest there were two friction igniters, fifteen or so quick-matches and a length of lunt. The rest of the equipment (2 ordinary vent-prickers, 2 vent-prickers with worms, 2 finger gloves, 4 drag ropes, 2 bags for the charge, 1 bag of quick-matches, 1 sheath for lances and 2 short shafts) was laid out over the chests.

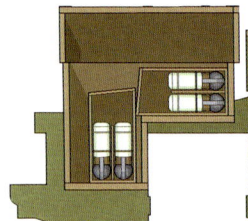
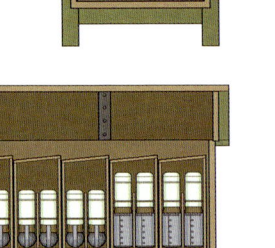
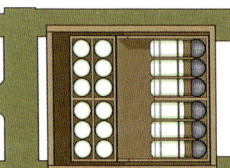
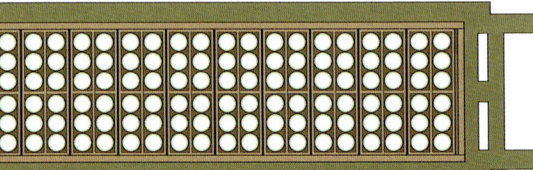

Cut-out view of the 6-pound caisson.

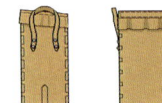

Views of the 6-pound watertight chest.

THE ARTILLERY TRAIN

Wagon driver in 1780, according to Leliepvre (see also the Driver after Hoffmann, reproduced on Plate 9 of Volume One). This civilian is wearing a blue cloth coat distinguished with iron grey.

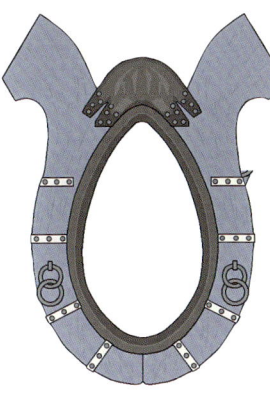

Collar painted blue during the *Ancien Regime*.

Driver in about 1793-1798, after Job. During the Revolutionary period, the drivers wore the peasant clothes of the region they came from with a military hat decorated with a tricolour cockade; they were armed with their whips.

Cart driver from the Breidt Company, wearing a blue cloth carmagnole, the dress he wore in Egypt in 1798, after Rigo. As Egypt forbade the placing of orders with civilian entrepreneurs, the general in chief, Bonaparte, organised a 12 company Artillery Train, or 902 men placed under the command of the *Adjudant-Major* Fabre.

Driver from the first Artillery Train formed with men taken from the various corps present in Egypt in about 1799-1801 after Rigo. With the scarcity of blue cloth, the Train was dressed in iron grey cloth, edged with dark blue. The colour of the cap's tuft is not known.

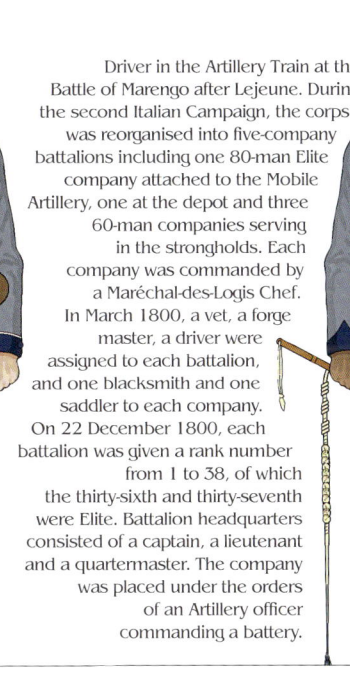

Driver in the Artillery Train at the Battle of Marengo after Lejeune. During the second Italian Campaign, the corps was reorganised into five-company battalions including one 80-man Elite company attached to the Mobile Artillery, one at the depot and three 60-man companies serving in the strongholds. Each company was commanded by a Maréchal-des-Logis Chef. In March 1800, a vet, a forge master, a driver were assigned to each battalion, and one blacksmith and one saddler to each company. On 22 December 1800, each battalion was given a rank number from 1 to 38, of which the thirty-sixth and thirty-seventh were Elite. Battalion headquarters consisted of a captain, a lieutenant and a quartermaster. The company was placed under the orders of an Artillery officer commanding a battery.

ARTILLERY TRAIN

Soldier in the Artillery Train wearing stable dress in about 1801-1804, with a jacket crossing over the chest with iron grey sleeves and blue distinctives, and white canvas trousers.

Driver in the Artillery Train wearing regulation dress in about 1802-1803, after Rousselot.

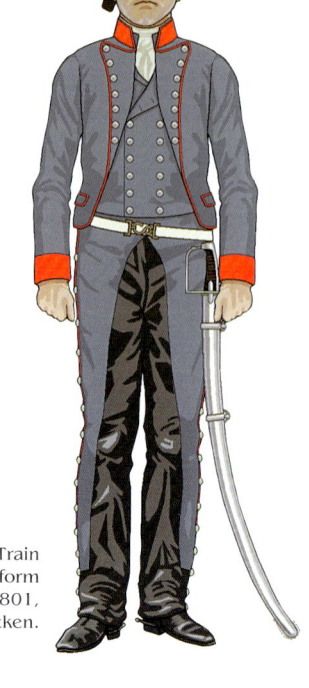

Driver in the Artillery Train wearing the first uniform introduced in 1801, after L. and F. Funcken.

Driver from the Artillery Train in An-VIII, after Job. The habit-veste had two shoulder flaps without edging, turnbacks without ornamentation and slanted pockets. According to Rousselot, the ordinary companies' pompon could be blue and red. The team horses belonged to the Republic. In peacetime, 1,000 mounts were kept for service whereas a large number of the horses were handed over to farmers under the supervision of the *Préfets*.

Soldier from Artillery Train wearing the first uniform, according to a drawing by Job. The red plume on the hat designates a man in the Elite Company.

THE ARTILLERY TRAIN

Soldier in the Artillery Train in working dress, comprising a smock and canvas trousers, and an iron grey forage cap.

On 4 August 1801 (16 thermidor An IX), the train was reorganised into 8 six-company battalions with at the headquarters: 1 captain *commandant*, 1 lieutenant *adjudant-major*, 1 sous-lieutenant quartermaster, 1 *adjudant* NCO, 1 Vet, 1 Master Trumpeter, 1 Master Saddler-Harnesser-Pack-Saddler, 1 Master Cobbler-Bootmaker, 1 Master-Tailor, and later on 1 Health Officer, 1 Forge Master and 1 Master-Armourer. The company consisted of 1 Lieutenant, 1 Sous-Lieutenant, 1 *Maréchal-des-Logis Chef*, 4 *Maréchaux-des-Logis*, 1 *Brigadier-Fourrier*, 5 *Brigadiers*, 59 soldiers, 2 blacksmiths, 2 pack-saddlers and 2 Trumpeters.

The first habit-veste recognised by the administration

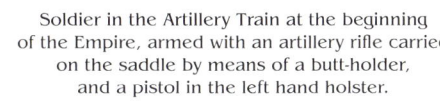

in 1801, made out of iron grey cloth, with dark blue lapels, facings and especially the collar.

Soldier in the Artillery Train at the beginning of the Empire, armed with an artillery rifle carried on the saddle by means of a butt-holder, and a pistol in the left hand holster.

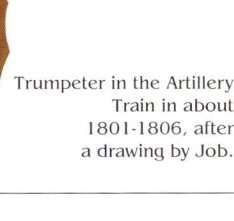

An VIII driver in the Artillery Train, after Job.

Trumpeter in the Artillery Train in about 1801-1806, after a drawing by Job.

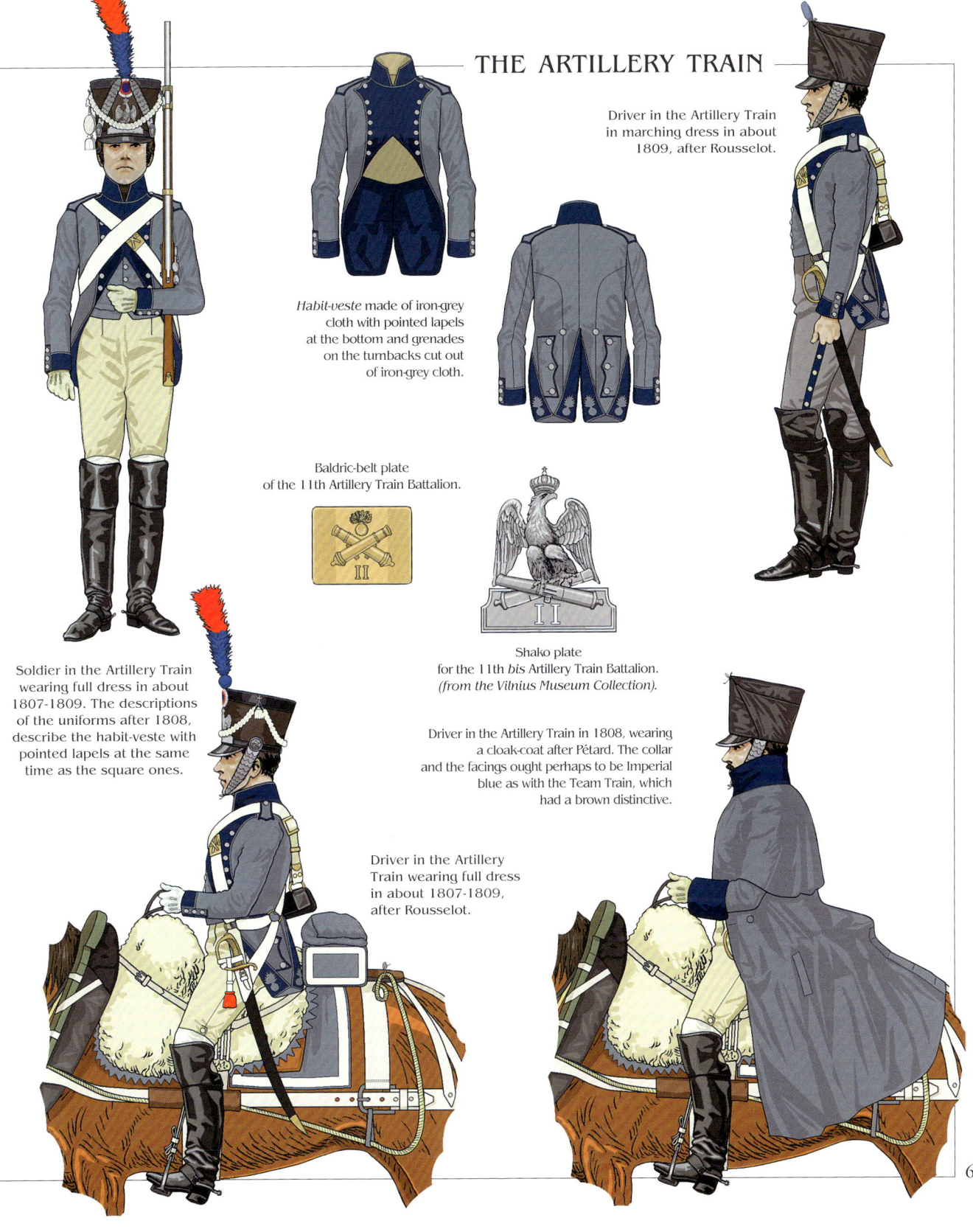

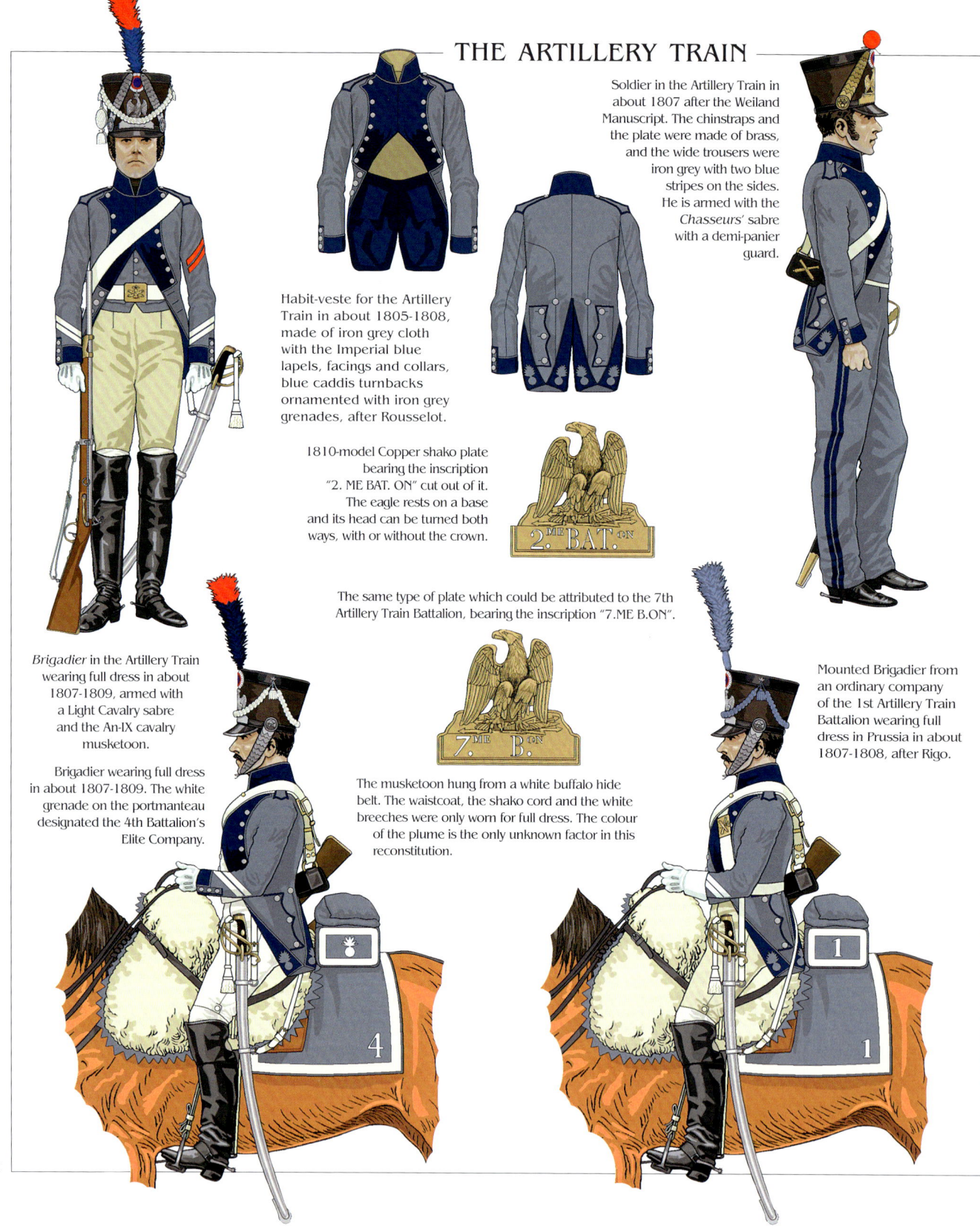

THE ARTILLERY TRAIN

Trumpeter from an ordinary company in the 2nd Artillery Train Battalion, wearing full dress in about 1807-1812. The centre of the pompon which is not visible here is dark blue with a white number. The stripes on the lapels, facings, collar and turnbacks were white or silver.

Trumpeter in the Artillery Train wearing a greatcoat in about 1807-1810. This reconstitution enables us to see that he is wearing the same items as the ordinary soldiers.

Trumpeter from the Horse Artillery Train of the Line in about 1807-1809, after the Carl Collection. We are in the presence of a man from the Elite Company. The colour of the instrument's cord is not clear on the original drawing.

Trumpeter from the Elite Company of an Artillery Train Battalion, in about 1806-1810, with the habit-veste colours reversed (reconstitution).

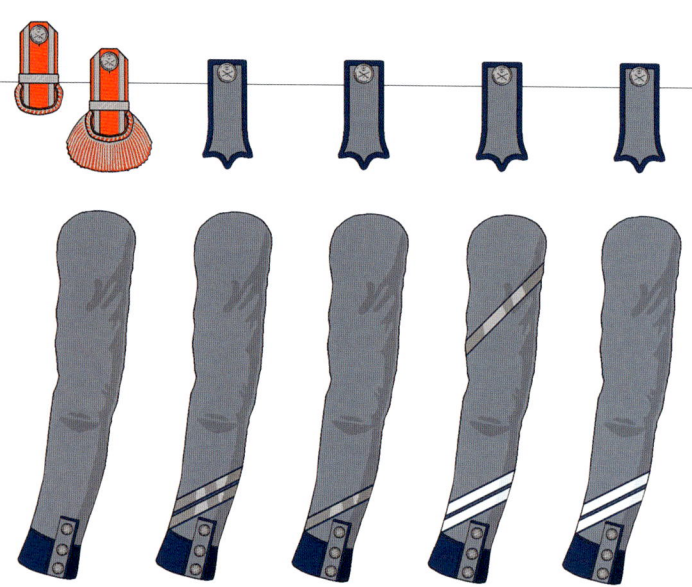

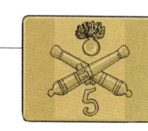

Two baldric-belt plates for the 5th Artillery Train Battalion. *(Musée de l'Armée Collection).*

Shako plate for the 4th *bis* Artillery Train Battalion as shown by the cut out inscription: 4ᵉ Bis.T.N D'ART. RIE.

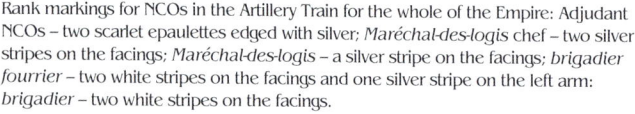

Rank markings for NCOs in the Artillery Train for the whole of the Empire: Adjudant NCOs – two scarlet epaulettes edged with silver; *Maréchal-des-logis* chef – two silver stripes on the facings; *Maréchal-des-logis* – a silver stripe on the facings; *brigadier fourrier* – two white stripes on the facings and one silver stripe on the left arm: *brigadier* – two white stripes on the facings.

Uniform button for the Artillery Train, made of melted white metal and decorated with two crossed cannon, a grenade and the battalion's number.

Shako plate for the 4th Artillery Train Battalion; this is the first model, in use until 1813. *(Musée de l'Armée Collection)*

Driver in the Artillery Train in 1807, after Vernet.

Driver in the Artillery Train wearing full dress in about 1807-1808, after Rousselot.

Veterinary surgeon in the 6th Artillery Train Battalion, before the 1812 Regulations, seen in *le Passepoil 1934*. He is wearing the uniform of a Horse Gunner and the stripes of a Maréchal-des-Logis, above strange facings with flaps on the dolman.

THE ARTILLERY TRAIN

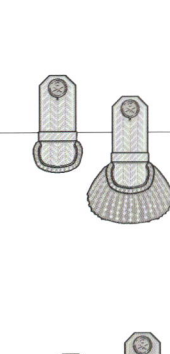

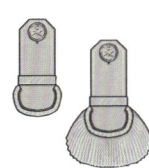

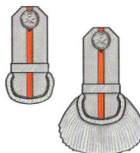

Lieutenant in the 1st Artillery Train Battalion wearing full dress in Prussia in about 1807-1808, after Rigo.

Officer wearing a frock coat in about 1806-1815 (reconstitution).

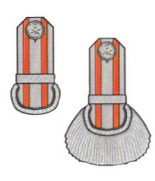

Squadron or battalion commander's epaulettes, captain *adjudant-major*'s epaulettes, second captain's epaulettes, lieutenant's epaulettes, sous-lieutenant's epaulettes.

Lieutenant at battalion headquarters in the Artillery Train in about 1806-1810 (reconstitution).

Lieutenant in the Horse Artillery train (elite) in marching dress in about 1806-1810, wearing grey trousers striped with silver or blue, for the circumstances.

THE ARTILLERY TRAIN

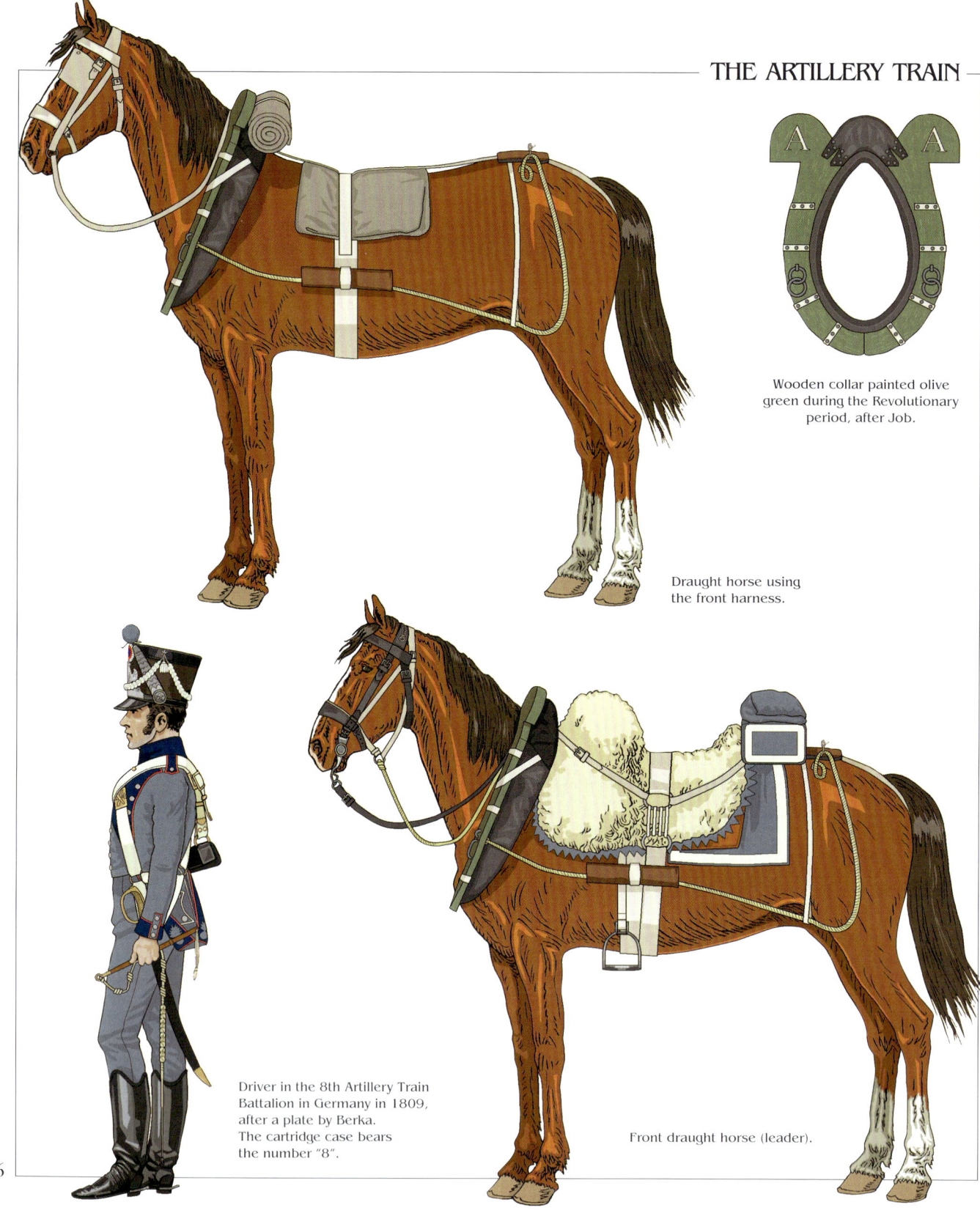

Wooden collar painted olive green during the Revolutionary period, after Job.

Draught horse using the front harness.

Driver in the 8th Artillery Train Battalion in Germany in 1809, after a plate by Berka. The cartridge case bears the number "8".

Front draught horse (leader).

THE ARTILLERY TRAIN

Officer wearing town summer dress in about 1810, after a miniature.

Artillery Train driver in Spain in 1809, after El Guil.

Soldier in the Artillery Train wearing an infantry greatcoat and a sky blue forage cap in about 1810-1812, after the tailoring estimates.

On 18 April 1810, a 14th ordinary battalion was formed with Dutch soldiers and took the 27th place in the Corps. On 29 June 1811 the 1st, 3rd, 6th, 7th, 7th bis, 8th, 8th bis, 9th, 11th and 14th Battalions each had their headquarters increased by 1 Battalion Commander, 1 *commandant*, 1 second captain-commanding (for two companies), 1 third lieutenant commanding (for the depot), 1 *adjudant-major*, 1 quarter-master treasurer, 2 *adjudants* NCOs, 1 vet, 1 forge master, 1 master trumpeter, 1 master-saddler and harnesser and 1 master cobbler-boot maker. The companies numbered 1 lieutenant or sous-lieutenant commanding, 1 *maréchal-des-logis* chef, 6 *maréchals-des-logis*, 1 *brigadier-fourrier*, 6 *brigadiers*, 2 Trumpeters, 2 blacksmiths, 2 harnessers-saddlers, 120 soldiers and 151 horses, of which 21 were saddled.

Sky blue "à la Kinski" Habit-veste with Imperial blue collar, facings and turnbacks, the piping and the grenades white, adopted by the Artillery Train after 1810, according to the tailoring quotations.

Soldier in the Artillery Train in 1811 wearing a sky blue "à la Kinski" coat with Imperial blue pointed facings, after a letterhead in the Glasser Collection.

Driver in the Artillery Train wearing a sky blue habit-veste, in about 1810-1811, after Rousselot.

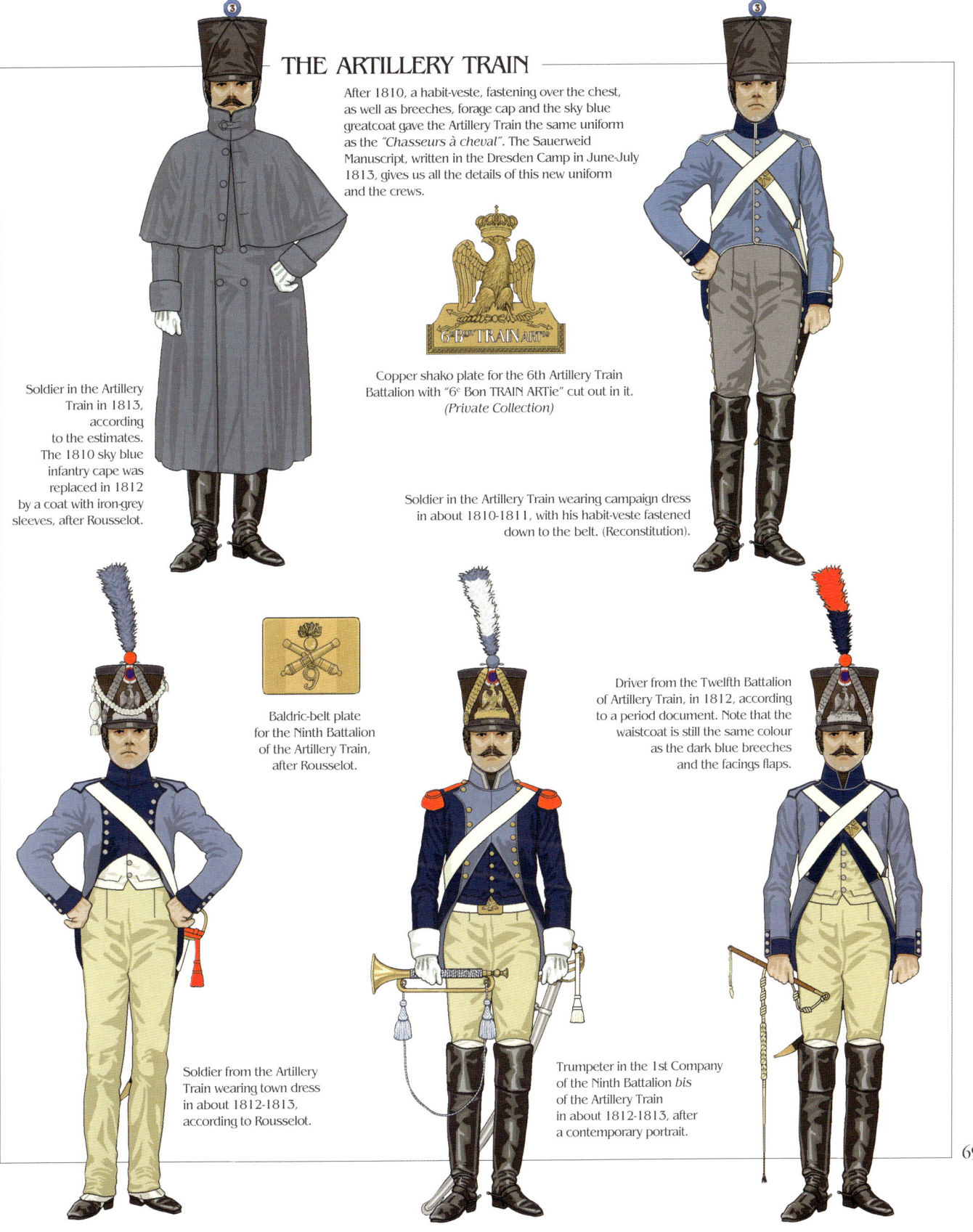

THE ARTILLERY TRAIN

After 1810, a habit-veste, fastening over the chest, as well as breeches, forage cap and the sky blue greatcoat gave the Artillery Train the same uniform as the *"Chasseurs à cheval"*. The Sauerweid Manuscript, written in the Dresden Camp in June-July 1813, gives us all the details of this new uniform and the crews.

Soldier in the Artillery Train in 1813, according to the estimates. The 1810 sky blue infantry cape was replaced in 1812 by a coat with iron-grey sleeves, after Rousselot.

Copper shako plate for the 6th Artillery Train Battalion with "6e Bon TRAIN ARTie" cut out in it. *(Private Collection)*

Soldier in the Artillery Train wearing campaign dress in about 1810-1811, with his habit-veste fastened down to the belt. (Reconstitution).

Baldric-belt plate for the Ninth Battalion of the Artillery Train, after Rousselot.

Driver from the Twelfth Battalion of Artillery Train, in 1812, according to a period document. Note that the waistcoat is still the same colour as the dark blue breeches and the facings flaps.

Soldier from the Artillery Train wearing town dress in about 1812-1813, according to Rousselot.

Trumpeter in the 1st Company of the Ninth Battalion *bis* of the Artillery Train in about 1812-1813, after a contemporary portrait.

THE ARTILLERY TRAIN

Sky-blue habit-veste with long skirts decorated with red grenades, for the Train officers in 1813, after Sauerweid.

Officer in the Foot Artillery Train in 1813, at the Dresden Camp, after Sauerweid.

Officer in the Artillery Train wearing a dark blue cape, according to Sauerweid's description, in 1813.

Officer in the Artillery Train wearing the Chasseurs à cheval uniform, at the Dresden Camp in 1813, after Sauerweid.

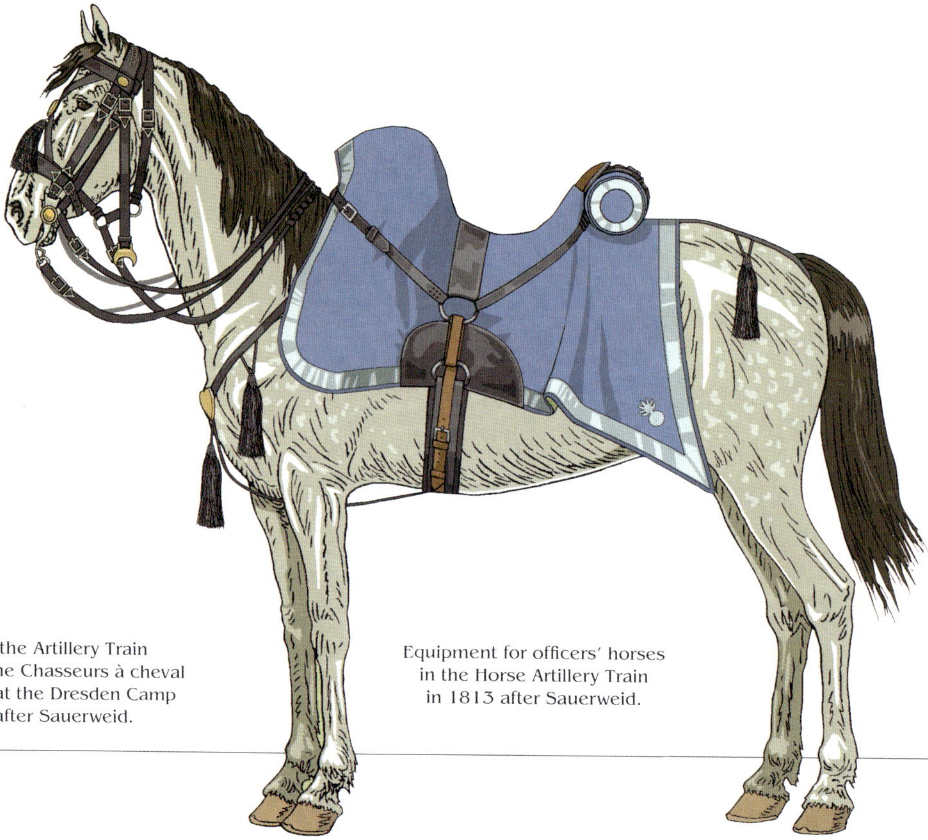

Equipment for officers' horses in the Horse Artillery Train in 1813 after Sauerweid.

THE ARTILLERY TRAIN

Officer from the Artillery Train wearing a blue coat, at Dresden in 1813, after Sauerweid's description.

Elite Company sky blue *habit-veste*, with Imperial Blue lapels, collar, turnbacks, facings and facing flaps edged with white, with red grenades after Sauerweid, in 1813.

Soldier in the Artillery Train wearing a completely sky blue cavalry coat with brigadier stripes on the sleeves.

Shako plate shown in Sauerweid's drawing.

Ordinary Company sky blue *habit-veste* in 1813, with white edging and grenades, after Sauerweid.

Officer from the Elite Artillery Train wearing campaign dress at the Dresden Camp, according to a drawing by Sauerweid.

Officer from Artillery Train wearing campaign dress at the Dresden Camp seen in 1813, by Sauerweid.

71

THE ARTILLERY TRAIN

Driver from the Artillery Train wearing campaign dress in 1813, according to Sauerweid. The grey breeches have sheepskin edged with red and the sabre is hanging from an infantry baldric.

Harnessing belonging to the leader horse, in the ordinary Companies of the Artillery Train at the Dresden Camp in 1813, according to Sauerweid.

Driver from the 3rd Artillery Train Battalion wearing full dress, at Dresden in 1813, according to the Sauerweid manuscript; he is shown with white breeches and an infantry sabre holder.

Harnessing belonging to the wheeler in the ordinary Companies of the Artillery Train at he Dresden Camp, in 1813 (reconstitution after Sauerweid).

THE ARTILLERY TRAIN

Horse Artillery train driver wearing campaign dress in 1813, after Sauerweid. The sky blue sheepskin overbreeches could be edged with blue or red stripes.

Harnessing for the leader, in the Elite Company of the Artillery Train at the Dresden Camp in 1813, according to Sauerweid.

Horse Artillery Train driver at the Dresden Camp in 1813, according to Sauerweid. This soldier is wearing Hungarian breeches and Light Cavalry boots edged with scarlet.

Harnessing belonging to the wheeler from the Elite Company in 1813 (reconstitution after Sauerweid).

THE ARTILLERY TRAIN

Worker in the Artillery Train wearing a knitted iron-grey infantry cape (reconstitution according to the organisation of the team trains).

Worker in the Artillery Train wearing working dress, in about 1812-1813.

Soldier in the Workers' Company of the Artillery Train in about 1812-1813. He is wearing sky blue epaulettes on an iron-grey *habit-veste* fastened down to the waist. The turnbacks are decorated with white grenades and the shako with a red pompom.

Lieutenant in the Artillery Train Workers, in about 1813-1814 (reconstitution).

Marshal Expert Worker in the Artillery Train with the rank of *Maréchal-des-Logis* wearing working dress in about 1813-1814 (reconstitution).

On 4 August 1801 (16 Thermidor of Year IX) a Worker's Company for the Train was created for wartime, joining the Army pool. It comprised 1 Sous-Lieutenant, 1 Maréchal-des-Logis, 1 *Brigadier-Fourrier*, a squad of saddlers (or three men per battalion), 1 Master-*Bourrelier Maréchal-des-Logis*, a squad of pack-saddle makers (2 men per battalion), 1 Master-Pack-Saddler *Maréchal-des-Logis*, a squad of marshals (two men per battalion), and 1 *Maréchal Expert Maréchal-des-Logis*. On 4 April 1812, a decree created once and for all the Worker Company for the Artillery Train.

Worker in the Artillery Train in about 1813-1814, armed with a rifle and its bayonet and a sabre; he is wearing the sky blue epaulettes and the red pompom of the Elite troops (reconstitution).

THE ARTILLERY TRAIN

Brigadier from the Artillery Train in marching dress in 1814. He is wearing the old shako decorated with the new plate, grey overbreeches without sheepskin (since 1812), according to the Elberfeld Manuscript.

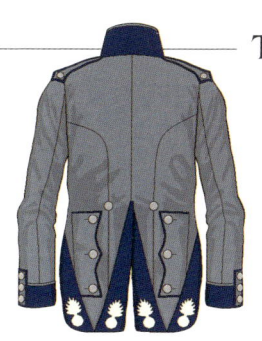

Habit-veste according to the 1812 Regulations, made of iron-grey cloth with Imperial blue lapels, the facings, turnbacks and collar, white grenades and shoulder flaps buttoned on the outside.

Driver from an ordinary Company in the Artillery Train in about 1813-1814, according to the 1812 Regulations, after Rousselot.

1812-model Artillery Train shako plate; the Battalion number has been cut out of the base.
(Musée de l'Armée Collection)

Driver from the Artillery Train wearing campaign dress, in about 1813-1814 (reconstitution).

Maréchal-des-logis from the 7th Artillery Train Battalion in about 1813-1814, according to the Bardin Regulations.

THE ARTILLERY TRAIN

Soldier in the Artillery Train wearing campaign dress in 1815, with the iron-grey jacket and the shako plate, decapitated during the First Restoration (reconstitution).

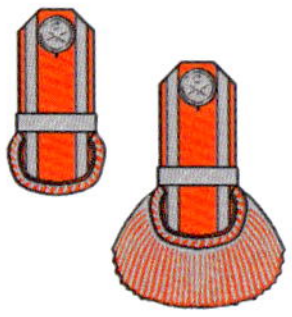

Maréchal-des-logis wearing campaign dress in about 1813-1814. He is wearing a silver ten years' service chevron. (reconstitution)

On 12 May 1814, during the First Restoration, the Artillery Train was reorganised into 4 squadrons of 271 men including 15 officers, with 120 horses, with the strength of the first eight battalions. On 9 September 1814, the corps was increased to 8 squadrons.

Adjudant sous-officer in about 1813-1814, (reconstitution after the 1812 Regulations). He is wearing a scarlet epaulette and counter-epaulette with two silver stripes and silver and scarlet fringes. The shako is decorated with a scarlet stripe with a line of silver and a white headquarters pompom.

Driver from the Artillery Train wearing a greatcoat made of iron-grey cloth, according to the 1812 Regulations, after Rousselot.

Soldier from the Artillery Train wearing a sleeveless waistcoat adopted with the new *habit-veste*. (reconstitution).

Brigadier from the Artillery Train wearing stable dress towards the end of 1813. He is wearing the new iron-grey jacket, shortened so as not to stick out from under the straight coat. The right hand pocket is open whereas the left hand one is fake. The rank and seniority markings on the habit-veste are set out in the same way as on the jacket.

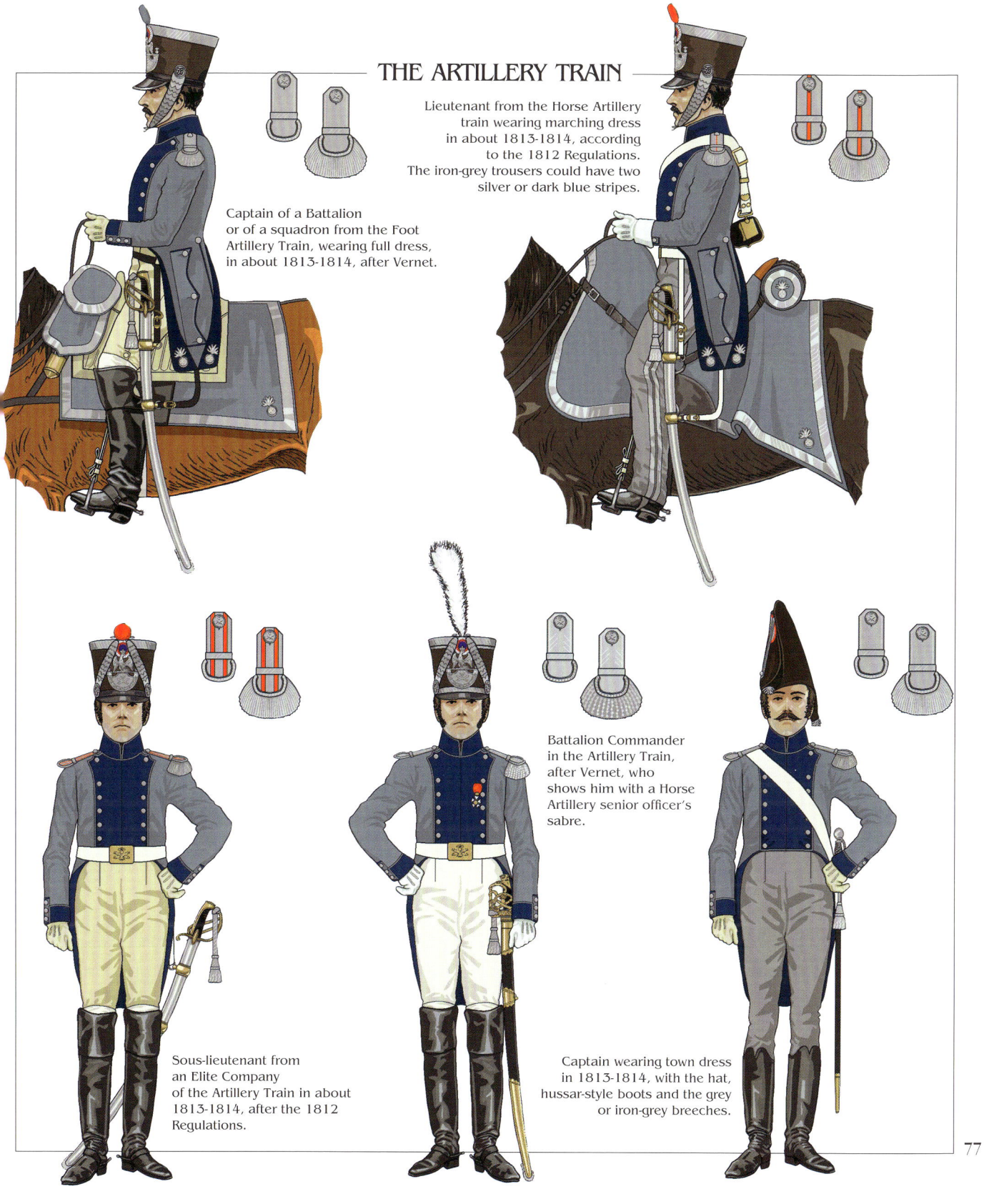

THE ARTILLERY TRAIN

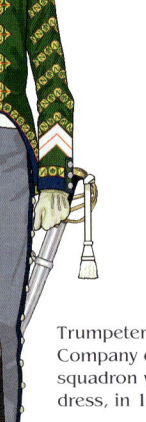

Trumpeter in the Artillery Train wearing exercise dress which should be made of green cloth edged with blue according to the 1812 Bardin Regulations.

Left and right-hand vertical and transversal stripes on the Imperial livery and common to all corps.

Trumpeter in the Artillery Train wearing exercise dress which should be made of green cloth edged with blue according to the 1812 Bardin Regulations.

Habit-veste of a Trumpeter of an Artillery Train squadron on the Imperial livery according the 1812 Regulation book.

Trumpeter in the Elite Company of an Artillery Train squadron wearing campaign dress, in 1814 (reconstitution).

Trumpeter in the Elite Company of an Artillery Train squadron wearing campaign dress, in 1814 (reconstitution).

THE ARTILLERY TRAIN

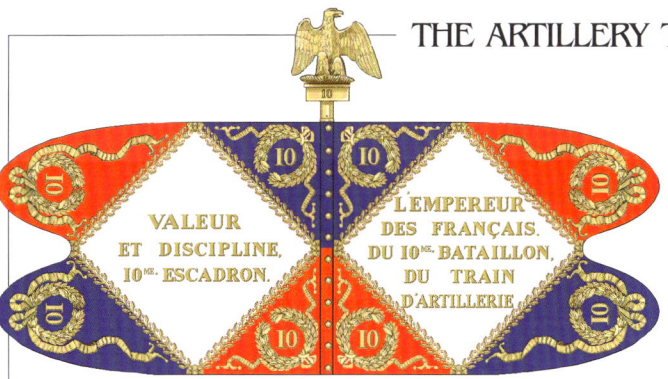

10th Artillery Train Battalion Pennant, cut in a single 31.50 by 23.62 inch thickness of silk, painted gold and shaded with brown. On the obverse side was embroidered: L'EMPEREUR/DES FRANCAIS./ DU 10 ME. BATTALION,/ DU TRAIN/D'ARTILLERIE and on the reverse side: VALEUR/ET DISCIPLINE,/ 10 ME ESCADRON (instead of Company), after the Brunon Collection.

Obverse side of the 9th Artillery Train Battalion pennant with the inscription: L'EMPEREUR/DES FRANCAIS./ DU 9. ME BATTALION/PAL DU TRAIN/ D'ARTILLERIE

At the beginning of the Empire, the Artillery Train received one Chaillot type 1804-model pennant for each of the ten battalions. Further pennants were ordered later on when the battalions doubled up. The recently created 11th, 12th, 13th and 14th Battalions do not seem to have received any pennants between 1806 and 1810.

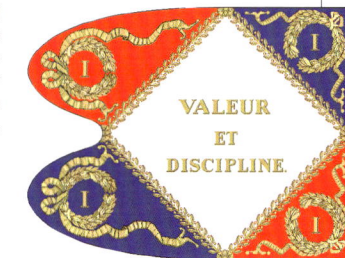

The single 1812-model standard for all the corps in the Artillery Train, with on the obverse side: L'EMPEREUR/NAPOLEON/AUX BATTALIONS/DU TRAIN/D'ARTILLERIE and on the reverse side all the names of the battles: ULM/AUSTERLITZ/ JENA/FRIEDLAND/ECKMÜHL/ ESSLING/WAGRAM (reconstitution).

1815-model Eagle and standard entrusted to the 1st Squadron of the Artillery Train *(Aspley House Collection, London)*. On the obverse side is embroidered: L'EMPEREUR/NAPOLEON/AU TRAIN/D'ARTILLERIE and on the reverse side all the names of the battles: ULM/AUSTERLITZ/ JENA/FRIEDLAND/ ECKMÜHL/ESSLING/ WAGRAM, after Charrié.

Pennant-bearer of the 1st Artillery Train Battalion in about 1804-1806, after Rigo. This is the *Maréchal-des-logis chef* of the Battalion's Elite Company. The obverse side bears the inscription: L'EMPEREUR/DES FRANCAIS,/ AU 1ER BATTALION/DU TRAIN/D'ARTILLERIE and the reverse side: VALEUR/ET/DISCIPLINE. *(Musée de l'Armée Collection)*

In 1812, all the eagles were withdrawn except the 1st Battalion's, which had remained at the depot with the first Inspector of Artillery; it was attached to the only standard of the Corps.

1815-model cravat and cord.

COMPOSITION OF A HORSE ARTILLERY DIVISION IN AN IX

Each Regiment had 6 Companies, totalling 40 officers, 534 Gunners and 38 guns. The regimental headquarters regrouped: 1 brigade commander, 1 squadron commander, 1 Quartermaster, 1 *Adjudant-Major*, 1 Adjudant NCO, 1 vet, 1 saddler, 1 boot-maker and 1 tailor. In each of the companies there were: 1 First Captain, 2 Second Captains, 1 First-Lieutenant, 2 Second-Lieutenants, 1 Maréchal-des-Logis Chef, 3 *Maréchaux-des-Logis*, 1 *Brigadier-Fourrier*, 3 *Brigadiers*, 2 Trumpeters, 1 woodworker, 1 blacksmith, 1 harnesser, 29 First Gunners and 49 Second Gunners.

The Company formed a division regrouping a battery of 27 carriages with 156 horses. The division had six guns, of which four were 8-pounders and two 6-pound howitzers (hitched to six horses), fourteen ammunition caissons, two per gun and three per howitzer (hitched to six horses), three chariots, of which one for the Company, one for the Train and one spare (hitched to six horses), two forges of which one for the Artillery (hitched to six horses), the second one was for the Train (hitched to four horses), two spare carriages, one for the 8-pounder and the other for the 6-pound howitzer (hitched to four horses). The Foot Artillery division comprised eight guns including two howitzers.

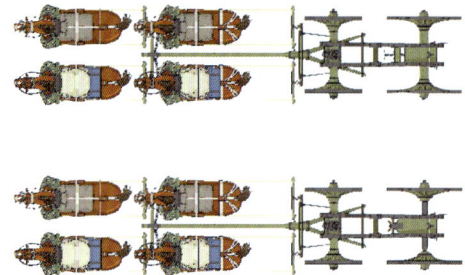

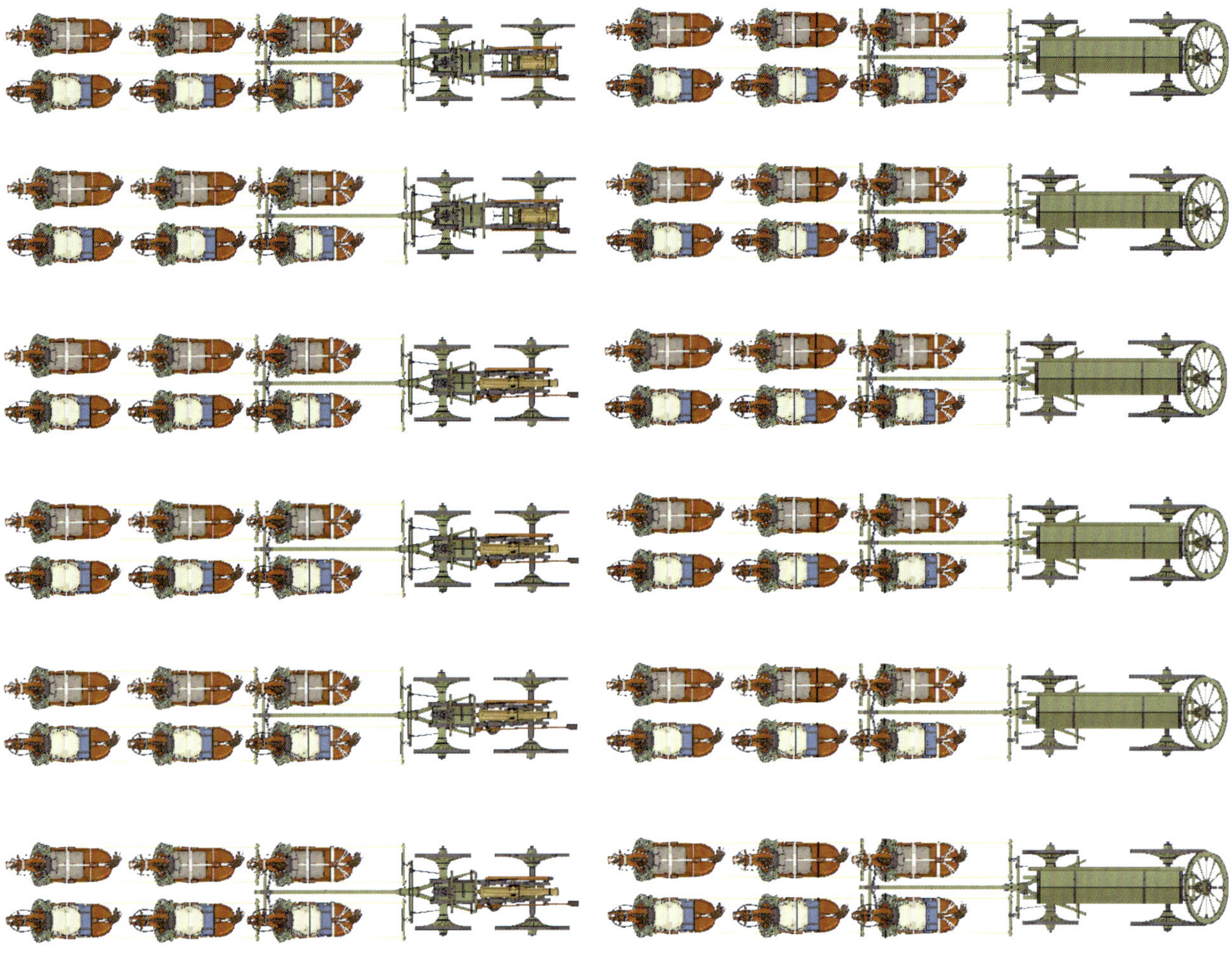

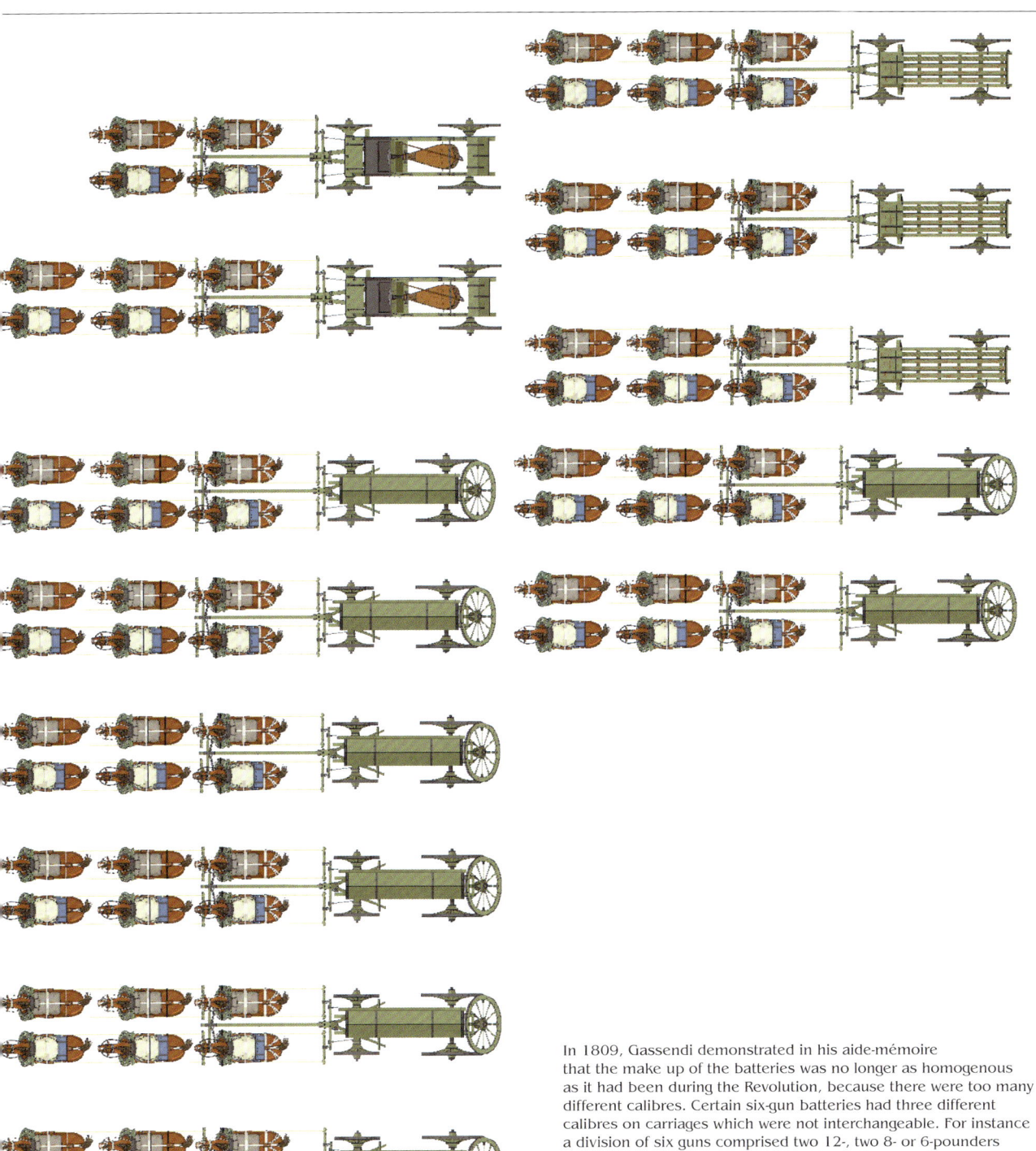

In 1809, Gassendi demonstrated in his aide-mémoire that the make up of the batteries was no longer as homogenous as it had been during the Revolution, because there were too many different calibres. Certain six-gun batteries had three different calibres on carriages which were not interchangeable. For instance a division of six guns comprised two 12-, two 8- or 6-pounders or two 6-inch howitzers, a spare carriage, sixteen caissons, two carts and one forge. The Horse Artillery was better balanced since it did not use any 12-pounders.

Sources and bibliography

— Volumes I and IV of "Règlement sur l'habit" from Bardin.

— *Le Plumet*. Plates nos 13, 76, 113,114, 164,169. Rigo. *Chez l'auteur.*

— L'Armée française. Plates from L. Rousselot Dedicated to the artillery of the line and the artillery of the Guard.

— L'uniforme et les armes des soldats du 1er Empire, L. et F. Funcken. *Casterman.*

— Équipement militaire de 1600 à 1870. Michel Pétard. *Chez l'auteur.*

— L'Artillerie Gribeauval. R. Ducoin. *Hors-série from CFFH.*

— L'Artillerie, de l'Ancien Régime à 1830. *Hors-série from carnets de la Sabretache.*

— Les uniformes de l'armée française. Dr Lienhart et R. Humbert. *Librairie Buhl.*

— Guide à l'usage des artistes et costumiers. H. Malibran.

— Plates from Martinet. Bertrand Malvaux. *Éditions du Canonnier.*

— Officers and soldiers. The Imperial Guard, volume I. André Jouineau, J.-M. Mongin. *Histoire & Collections.*

— Officers and soldiers. The Imperial Guard, volume V. André Jouineau. *Histoire & Collections.*

— Le canonnier à cheval. Michel Pétard. *Uniformes* n° 43

— Le canonnier à pied de la Garde. Michel Pétard in *Uniformes* n° 69.

— L'artillerie du Premier Empire. *Tradition magazine*, special issue n° 78-79.

Design and Layout by Ludovic Letrun — Book executed by the Studio "Éditions des Soixante", supervised by Jean-Marie Mongin for Histoire & Collections
© HISTOIRE & COLLECTIONS 2015

All rights reserved.
No part of this publication may be transmitted or reproduced without the written consent of the publisher.

ISBN: 978-2-35250-396-5

Publisher's number: 35250

© Histoire & Collections 2015

A BOOK PUBLISHED BY
HISTOIRE & COLLECTIONS
5, AVENUE DE LA RÉPUBLIQUE
75011 PARIS - FRANCE
Tel: +33 (0) 1 40 21 18 20
Fax: +33 (0) 1 47 00 51 11
www.histoireetcollections.com

Print by *Calidad Grafica* in Spain, European Union, in June 2015.